SEO FITNESS WORKBOOK:

The Seven Steps to Search Engine Optimization Success on Google

3RD EDITION

by Jason McDonald, Ph.D.
© 2014, JM InternetGroup
www.jm-seo.org

Table of Contents

Introduction 1

Attitude 12

Goals 19

Basics 25

Keywords 30

Keyword Worksheet 42

Page Tags 50

Website Structure 60

SEO Audit 70

Content SEO 75

Press Releases 82

Blogging 88

Links 93

Social Media 101

Local SEO 110

Metrics 116

Learning 123

Introduction

Welcome to the *SEO Fitness Workbook!* This workbook explains how to succeed at *Search Engine Optimization (SEO)* in **seven steps**.

SEO, of course, is the art and science of getting your company to the top of Google's organic (free) results. **Why is SEO so valuable?** Simply put, SEO is valuable because customers turn to Google first to find new products and services, new companies and consultants.

Everybody uses Google!

(*Well, a few people use Bing, but the game is the same. Rest assured that all techniques covered in this Workbook apply equally to Bing*).

The question for you is: when a customer does a relevant keywords search, does your company appear on the first page of Google results? Are you displayed in the top three "Olympic" positions (Gold / No. 1, Silver/ No. 2, Bronze / No 3), or at least on page one (top ten results)... or are you not on Google at all? If your customers use Google, and your website doesn't rank on page one, you need SEO! If Google is important to your Internet marketing, you need SEO!

Recall that SEO is the art and science of getting to the top of Google's organic search results. SEO is how to get free advertising on Google. SEO is the art and science of getting Google to drive qualified web traffic to your website, where those clicks become sales leads.

But isn't SEO hard?

Well, that's what Google would like you to think (so spend money on AdWords…) And that's what many in the SEO industry would like you to think (so pay us big consulting fees, and don't ask any questions!)

I don't agree. SEO isn't easy, but it isn't exactly hard either.

I've taught thousands of people in my online classes, in classes in the San Francisco Bay Area, and in corporate workshops, and I can confirm there is a lot of confusion about SEO. People think it's hard, or impossible, or mysterious, and that's simply not correct.

SEO, you see, is a lot like **physical fitness**. Although everyone can conceivably run a marathon, for example, few people make the effort to learn how and even fewer take the disciplined steps necessary to train for and ultimately finish a marathon. Does that make running a marathon easy? No. But does that make running a marathon hard?

Not really. Like running a marathon, SEO is **conceptually** simple (*exercise a lot, train with discipline, don't give up*) but practically hard (*you have to work at it nearly every day*).

And, of course, the Olympic champions don't just work *hard*, they work *smart*.

That's the beginning of the good news. If you just learn how to work smarter (not harder), you'll find that SEO isn't really that hard. And it gets better.

In most industries, you'll find that your competitors are not that smart. Most industries are not as competitive in SEO as you would think, and metaphorically speaking, you don't have to run faster than the bear; you just have to run faster than your buddy!

SEO = GOOGLE FITNESS

Fitness takes determination, discipline, and knowledge. This workbook guides you through the **seven steps** to successful SEO. Along the way, we'll set goals, understand technical details, and have fun. Along the way, I will be your "fitness coach" to explain how it all works and to motivate you to keep trying. **You can do this!**

To see SEO in action, launch your web browser, go to Google (http://www.google.com), and enter a few of the following search terms:

> SEO Class
> SEO Training Course Online
> SEO Training NYC
> How to get your picture on Google Search?
> What is Web spam?

You'll see the JM Internet Group (*jm-seo.org*) on page one of Google, and often at the top of these search results, and you'll usually see my picture (Jason McDonald) there as well. The methodology? The **Seven Steps to SEO Fitness**, the methodology you'll learn in this book!

Isn't that cool? I think it is. And, if I can do it for the JM-SEO.org and JasonMcDonald.org, you can do it for your business, too!

Throughout this workbook, I will share with you other examples of businesses that understand SEO and succeed using the **seven steps**.

SEO = FREE ADVERTISING ON GOOGLE

Before we get started, a few words about the SEO industry. Back to metaphors: the SEO industry is a lot like the fitness and diet industry.

How so?

Just as the diet and fitness industry is plagued with the latest crazy diet schemes such as strange nutritional supplements and other nonsense vs. the tried and true techniques of eating less and exercising more, so the SEO industry is plagued with fraud, crazy schemes, and all sorts of nonsense. Does that make SEO impossible? No, not at all. It just means that you must keep your wits about you, and follow a method that is clear, consistent, and based on facts.

Beware of hucksters promising quick success via shadowy tools! **Scams, schemes**, and **scoundrels** abound in the SEO ecosystem. (Doesn't that sound like the diet and fitness industry?)

What else is common in the diet and fitness industry? **Guilt** and **intimidation**. Just as many in the diet and fitness industry would like you to feel bad about yourself, to feel you "can't succeed" without their "magic pill," or their "secret knowledge" ... so the SEO industry is full of obnoxious computer nerds who seem to thrive on putting mere marketers and small business owners down. *You're stupid*, they say. *Feel guilty* you "don't get it," they say.

They want you to feel stupid, so you don't challenge their authority. *They* want you to feel powerless, so those checks keep coming.

Oh, and another thing about the diet industry. It's in a symbiotic relationship with the food industry: they sell us Big Macs and Mac N Cheese, and then they sell us diets to get off of them.

There is a symbiosis in the SEO industry as well. The SEO gurus along with Google attempt to convince us that SEO is an incredibly difficult, mystical skill... and then the same SEO gurus sell us expensive, esoteric services, while Google sells us AdWords advertising.

Google doesn't want you to understand SEO (which costs you **nothing**, and makes Google **nothing**). Google wants you to believe SEO is impossible, so you spend your money on Google advertising, i.e. AdWords.

GOOGLE HATES SEO
AND LOVES ADWORDS

I respectfully disagree with my friends in Mountain View, California, and my friends in the SEO industry.

I want you to feel **powerful** and **intelligent**. I want you to **succeed at SEO.**

The **seven steps to SEO fitness** are built on a philosophy of empowerment. Can you understand SEO? Yes you can! Can you implement SEO? Yes you can! It takes some knowledge, it takes some effort, but yes you can do it.

I am going to teach you how in seven **simple steps**.

Let's get started!

>> Meet the Author

My name is Jason McDonald, and I have been active on the Internet since 1994 and teaching SEO, AdWords, and Social Media since 2009 – online, in San Francisco, at Stanford University Continuing Studies, at workshops, and in corporate trainings. Over 1700 people have taken my paid trainings; over 19,000 my free webinars. I love figuring out how things work, and I love teaching others! SEO is an endeavor that I understand, and I want to empower you to understand it as well. Learn more about me at http://www.jasonmcdonald.org or at my corporate website http://www.jm-seo.org.

>> Why This Book is Different

There are quite a few books on SEO out there! There are zillions of blog posts! There are thousands of SEO consultants! There are hundreds of crazy harebrained schemes...

But there is only one **workbook**: the *SEO Fitness Workbook.*

How is a *workbook* different from a *book*? Here's how.

First of all, this workbook speaks in **practical, no-nonsense English.** Whereas most of the SEO books out there are *by* experts *for* experts, this workbook explains SEO in plain English and does not get lost in the details. Most businesspeople don't need to know every gory detail about SEO; rather they need practical, hands-on advice about what to do first, second, third and so forth.

Secondly, the SEO Fitness *Workbook* is **hands-on**. Most SEO books are meant to be passively read. SEO Fitness *Workbook*, by contrast, gives you "hands on" worksheets and deliverables. In fact, each chapter ends with a deliverable marked in red. Each chapter also has TODOS (marked in RED) because a workbook is not just about reading, it's about **doing** and **succeeding.**

Third, while most books are outdated on the day they are published, the SEO Fitness Workbook connects to lively **Internet resources** such as free SEO tools and hands-on YouTube videos that show you how to succeed. After all, in the 21st century, a "how to" book should be more than a book, shouldn't it? It should be a gateway to Internet knowledge.

Take a moment to check out all the online resources, including the companion *SEO Toolbook*, at http://www.jm-seo.org/promo with password: *fitness*.

Last but not least, watch a few of my YouTube videos; you'll find I am as crazy and enthusiastic on video as I am in this book!

>> Who This Book is for

I have written *SEO Fitness Workbook* for the following groups of practical business folk:

Small Business Owners. If you own a small business that gets (or could get) significant customer traffic from the Web, this book is for you.

Small Business Marketers. If you are in charge of marketing for a small business that gets (or could get) significant customer traffic from the Web, this book is for you.

Marketing Managers. If you lead a Web team of inside or outside bloggers, SEO content writers, or other Internet marketing technicians including external SEO companies, this book is for you.

Web Designers. If you design websites but want to design sites that not only look good but actually succeed at Google search, this book is for you.

Non-profit Marketers. If you work at a non-profit or governmental agency that depends on Web search traffic, then this book is also for you.

Anyone whose organization (and its products, services, or other offerings) would benefit from being at the top of Google, for free, can benefit from the *SEO Fitness Workbook.*

▶▶ The Seven Steps to SEO Fitness

1. Set the right **expectations**.

2. Identify your **keywords**.

3. **(Re)structure** your website.

4. Create **content**.

5. Go **social**.

6. **Measure** your results.

7. Never stop **learning**.

And here are the seven steps to SEO fitness in more detail –

Step #1: SET the right expectations. SEO, like physical fitness, is not something achieved in a day! It takes a "can do" attitude in addition to some knowledge to succeed.

1.1 Attitude – attitude is everything, and SEO requires a commitment to learning how SEO works as well as a desire to implement positive SEO-friendly changes.

1.2 Goals – define what you sell, who your customers are, and how best to reach them.

1.3 Basics – understand the basics of SEO, i.e. "on page" and "off page" tactics.

Step #2 IDENTIFY your keywords. Keywords drive nearly every aspect of SEO, so you need a well structured, clearly defined "keyword worksheet."

> **2.1 Keywords** – identify high volume, high value keywords.

> **2.2 Keyword Worksheet** – build a keyword worksheet and measure your rank on Google and Bing.

Step #3 (RE)STRUCTURE your website. Once you know your keywords, where do you put them? It begins with page tags, proceeds through website organization, and ends with an "SEO audit" that outlines your SEO strategy.

> **3.1 Page Tags** - weave your target keywords into your HTML Page Tags.

> **3.2 Website Structure** – build landing pages, restructure your home page, and optimize website layout.

> **3.3 SEO Audit** – now that you know the basics of "on page" SEO, conduct an "on page" SEO audit of your website.

Step #4 CREATE content. They say that "content is king" in terms of SEO, and they are right. In this section, you'll create a long-term content strategy that moves beyond the "quick fix" of your site to a day-by-day, week-by-week system of SEO-friendly content.

> **4.1 Content SEO** – devise a content strategy, specifically who will do what, when, where, how, and how often – that is, a short and long term SEO content marketing strategy.

> **4.2 Press Release SEO** - leverage news and free syndication services for SEO, because press releases are an easy technique to get links and build buzz on social media.

> **4.3 Blogging** – set up a blog that follows best SEO practices, including all-important connections to social media platforms like Google+ and Twitter.

Step #5 GO social. "Off page" SEO leverages external web links and social media to boost your website's authority on Google. Use the traditional tactic of getting relevant inbound links. Then, leverage social media platforms like Twitter, Google+, Facebook, LinkedIn and YouTube to enhance your SEO efforts!

5.1 Link Building – conduct a link building audit and create a long-term link building strategy.

5.2 Social Media SEO – look for social media mention opportunities, and enable relevant social profiles to enhance Google's trust in your website as an authoritative resource.

5.3 Local Optimization – local SEO stands at the juncture of SEO, local, and review based marketing.

Step #6 MEASURE your results. Like physical fitness, SEO is a process that starts with a defined set of goals and employs specific measurements about goal achievement.

6.1 Metrics - measure your progress towards the top of Google, inbound keywords, and paths taken by customers once they land on your website.

Step #7 NEVER stop learning. SEO starts with self-discovery, proceeds through technical knowledge, and ends with the hard work of implementation.

7.1 Online Materials – use Chapter 7 to get access to companion **worksheets**, **quizzes**, and the very important *SEO Toolbook,* which provides hundreds of free SEO tools, which can help you in all aspects of SEO, from identifying keywords through page tags to links and social mentions.

▶▶ Online Materials

The *SEO Workbook* embraces the Web, and is full of informative web links and videos. These are indicated in the text as blue links. (If you are reading in Kindle format, they are clickable). If not, go to http://www.jm-seo.org/workbook, where you can register your copy for free and gain access to online clickable chapter links.

If you have any problems, email info@jm-seo.org or call 510-713-2150 for help.

▶▶ Free SEO Dashboard – Stay up to date!

There's a lot to learn! I want to encourage you to be a "lifelong learner," so in addition to the chapter Web links and companion *SEO Toolbook*, I produce a free **SEO Dashboard**, listing the top, free learning resources for staying up-to-date on SEO.

To get the free *SEO Dashboard*, all I ask is that you write a candid review about *SEO Fitness Workbook* on Amazon.com. Then, simply go to the URL below, follow the instructions, and you'll receive access to my easy-to-use *SEO Dashboard*, my launch pad to the best SEO tools I use on a daily basis.

http://www.jm-seo.org/offer

Thanks in advance!

▶▶ Copyright and Disclaimer

▶▶ Acknowledgements

No man is an island, including me. I would like to thank my beloved wife, Noelle Decambra, for helping me hand-in-hand as the world's best moderator for our online classes, and as my personal cheerleader in the book industry. Gloria McNabb has done her usual tireless job as first assistant, including updating the *SEO Toolbook*. Alexander Facklis helped immensely with proofing and content as did Dianne Needham and Ray Williams, two participants in my Stanford Continuing Studies class.

And a huge thank you to my students – online, in San Francisco, and at Stanford Continuing Studies. You challenge me, you inspire me, and you motivate me!

Attitude

Most books on SEO start with the technical details. What's a TITLE tag? How do you understand your Google PageRank? Which factors in the Google algorithm have changed recently? We'll get to all that, but I want to start this book with a pep talk about: **Attitude**. *Attitude, they say, is everything*. And nowhere is that more true than in SEO. This is an industry full of information overload, pretty rude intimidators of a technical geeky type, and an 800 lb Gorilla (Google), that would really rather you just spend money on AdWords than understand how you can get to the top of Google without paying it a penny.

To succeed, you'll need a positive, "can do" attitude.

Let's get Started!

TO DO LIST:

>> Learn from Francie Baltazar-Schwartz that "Attitude is Everything"

>> Identify "Can Do" vs. "Can't Do" People

>> Learn to Measure

>> Deliverable: Inventory Your Team & Get Ready

>> Francie Baltazar-Schwartz and

Attitude is Everything

The Internet is a wonderful place, and Google sits pretty much at the center of it. Got a question? "Just *Google* it!" We certainly know the reality of "Just *Google* it" in terms of customers look for companies, products and services. But it also goes for more important questions like the *meaning of life (42), and what is a LOL cat,* anyway?

For example, Google "Who said 'Attitude is Everything?'" and you'll find out that this quote is attributed to one Francie Baltazar-Schwartz. Regardless of whether she did, or did not, actually say this, there is an article going round the Internet called "Atttitude is everything." You can read it at http://bit.ly/a-i-e. The point of "attitude is everything" is that you have two choices every day: either to have a **positive**, can-do attitude or to have a **negative**, can't do attitude.

This relates very dramatically to success at SEO, just as it does to success in pretty much everything else in life from physical fitness to your job to your marriage.

How does it apply to SEO? Well, let's look at the facts and let's look at the ecosystem of people and companies in the SEO industry.

Fact No. 1. SEO is technical, and at least on the surface, seems pretty complicated and hard. So, if you start out with the attitude that you "can't do it," you're already on the path to defeat. If, in contrast, you start with the attitude that you can do it, that other people are clearly doing it, you're on the path to success. **Attitude is everything.**

Fact No. 2. Google does not want anyone to believe that SEO is easy. Google is a multibillion dollar corporation and makes nearly 97% of its revenues off of paid advertising via AdWords. **Google wants you to believe that SEO is hard so that you spend money on AdWords.** And Google has a big, powerful marketing machine to propagate this message. If you are intimidated by Google, you're already on the path to defeat. If, in contrast, you have some healthy skepticism about Google (and big corporations in general), remembering that they are just people too, you're on the path to success. **Attitude is everything.**

Fact No. 3. The SEO industry is full of so-called experts, gurus, tools providers and others who pretty much make their money by intimidating normal folk into believing that SEO is incredibly complicated and only nerds with Ph.D's in computer science can do it. They want you to stay in a state of dependency and keep paying them the big bucks... So if you allow technical nerds to intimidate you, you're already on the path to defeat. If, in contrast, you realize that they aren't really any smarter than you and that SEO isn't just about technology, it's about words and concepts and marketing messages, you're on the path to success. **Attitude is everything.**

Oh, and as SEO becomes more and more social, you'll want to have an open mind about social media as well. You can really get yourself motivated by watching a 3rd grader (!) called "Kid President" who has YouTube videos with over 20 million views and was actually invited to the White House.

VIDEO. Watch a "Can Do" attitude video by "Kid President" at http://jm-seo.org/2999-t.

For your first **TODO**, therefore, concentrate your mind and create a **positive attitude:** this is going to be fun, this is going to be educational, this is going to be a journey! Your **attitude is everything** as to whether you'll succeed or fail at SEO!

If a third grader can get 23 million views and meet the President, don't you think you can at least get to page one of Google?

▶▶ Identify "Can Do" VS "Can't Do" People

In most situations, you'll need to depend on other people. Now the attitude of the people in your team (your webmaster, your content writers, your product marketing managers, your executives...) is also incredibly important. Are they "can do" or "can't do" sort of folks?

Henry Ford, the great industrialist, once made this clear observation:

> "Whether you think you can, or you think you can't--you're right."
> — Henry Ford

In terms of SEO, there are those people who think that a) they can't learn it, or b) it can't be done. And, guess what: they're **right**. And there are those who think that a) they can learn it, and b) it can be done. And, guess what: they're **right**, too.

Which camp are you in? Your team members? Can, or can't?

So for your second **TODO**, look around your organization and make a list of those people who need to be involved with your SEO project. For example:

Management and Marketers. These people are involved in the sense of understanding who your customers are, what you sell, and what the sales objectives are for your website. Your website, after all, isn't an end in itself but a means to an end: more sales.

Content Writers. Who writes (or will write) content for the website? These people need at least a basic understanding of your keywords and, even better, an understanding of how "on page" SEO works so that they know where to strategically place keywords on web content.

Web Designers. News flash: your website isn't just for humans! It's also for Google. You'll have to educate your web design team that your website needs to "talk" to Google just as much as it "talks" to humans. As we will learn, what Google likes (text) isn't generally what people like (pictures).

Web Programmers. The folks who program the backend, like your URL structure, your XML sitemaps and all that technical stuff. Who are these people and how will you get them on board for the SEO project?

Social Media Experts. Social media is the new wave in SEO, so you'll need those folks who are (or will be) active on Twitter, Google+, YouTube, Facebook and the like to be "SEO aware," in the sense of how social media impacts SEO performance.

Indeed, if you have some really obstructionist "Can't Do" people, you'll need to strategize either how to a) persuade them to participate, b) get out of the way, or c) work around them.

>> Learn to Measure

As you assemble your team, you'll want to get their buy in on learning SEO. It isn't a rocket science, but it's also not something you'll learn in a day. First, they'll need to learn the basics (See Chapter 1.3). Second, they'll need to learn many of the more esoteric topics as needed. Content writers, for example, will need to be keenly aware of keywords and how to write semantically friendly SEO text. Web programmers will need to understand XML sitemaps and so on. Third, they'll need to be committed to lifelong learning, as SEO does change over time. A good strategy is to schedule monthly meetings or corporate email exchanges about your SEO progress.

Let's also talk a little about **measurement** and **metrics**. One of the biggest stumbling blocks to successful SEO is the idea that it can't be measured. It can. How so?

Know your keywords. Once you know your keywords, as you'll learn in Chapter 2.1, then you can start to measure your rank on target Google searches.

Inbound search traffic. Once you set up Google Analytics properly as you'll learn in Chapter 6.1, you can measure your inbound "organic" traffic from Google, including separating branded from non-branded traffic. This answers the question of are you pulling traffic from Google, and via what keywords.

Goals. Every good website should have defined goals, usually registrations and/or sales. Once you define goals in Google Analytics, you can track where your traffic comes from and what traffic converts.

When you first start, you'll often have little idea of your target keywords, little idea of your rank on Google, and little idea of your traffic patterns from landings to conversions. But that doesn't mean SEO isn't a measurable activity! It just means you are not yet measuring.

Why is this important? As you set up your team, and establish the right attitude, you want to establish the idea that SEO is measurable. If someone has crazy ideas (like Google doesn't pay attention to URL structure, or keywords don't matter), you can measure these ideas vs. correct ideas (keywords in TITLE tags matter a great deal, keyword-heavy URL's help a lot). Establishing a culture of measurability will help you get everyone on your team, even the most recalcitrant "Can't Do" people to realize that SEO works, and SEO can get your website to actually generate sales or sales leads.

Measurability is a critical part of Step No. 1: **Setting the Right Expectations.**

▶▶ Deliverable: Inventory Your Team & Get Ready

Now we've come to the end of Step 1.1, your first **DELIVERABLE** has arrived. Open up a Word document and create a list of all the people who are involved with your website, from the marketing folk who identify the goals (sales or registrations?), to the content writers (those who create product descriptions, blog posts, or press releases), to the Web design people (graphic designers), to the Web programmers. Make an inventory of who needs to be involved in what aspects of SEO, and if possible, set up weekly or monthly meetings about your SEO strategy.

At a "top secret" level, you might also want to indicate who has a "Can Do" and who has a "Can't Do" attitude. You'll want to work to bring everyone over into the "Can Do" column!

Goals

SEO, like physical fitness, can't be accomplished without **goals**. Are you training for a marathon, or a sprint? Want to look better at the beach, or just be healthier? Want to dominate Google for "industrial fan" or "organic baby food?" SEO can tell you how to get to the top of Google, but it can't tell you *what* your company's *goals* are vis-à-vis potential customers. To succeed at SEO, you need to have a clear vision of your *sales ladder* starting at the customer need and then proceeding to: keyword search *query* — *landing* on your website — sales *inquiry* — *back* and *forth* — actual *sale*.

Let's get started!

TO DO LIST:

>> Define Your Business Value Proposition

>> Identify Your Target Customers by Segment

>> Establish Marketing Goals

>> Deliverable: a Goals Worksheet

>> Define Your Business Value Proposition

What does your business sell? Who wants it, and why? Sit down and write a *business value proposition (BVP)* for your business. A BVP is a sentence or short paragraph that succinctly defines what a business does and the value that it provides to customers.

For a New York watch repair shop such as Ron Gordon Watch Repair (http://www.rongordonwatches.com) , the business value proposition is that it provides watch repair services to people living or working in Manhattan who need to get their luxury watches (e.g., Tag Heuer, Breitling, Hamilton) repaired quickly and easily.

For an industrial fan company like Industrial Fans Direct (http://www.industrialfansdirect.com), the business value proposition might be to provide quality industrial fans for harsh environments such as factories or farms. For a Las Vegas commercial real estate broker, it might be that the company helps businesses in the Las Vegas area identify great commercial, warehouse, and retail space for rent in the best locations at the best prices. For a Miami divorce attorney, it might be efficient, effective representation in divorce proceedings for high income individuals with children.

For any business, a *business value proposition* is your "elevator pitch" to a potential customer - what do they want, and what do you have?

> For your first **TODO**, open up a Word document and write a sentence or short paragraph that succinctly defines what your business does and how it provides value for customers. For the worksheet, go to http://bit.ly/mvp-word (Word) or http://bit.ly/mvp-pdf (PDF).

▶▶ Identify Your Target Customers by Segment

Your business value proposition explicitly describes the relationship between what you provide and what they want. Now dig deeper: segment your customers into definable groups. For instance, Ron Gordon Watch Repair might segment its customers into the following:

- Manhattan office workers seeking quick and convenient repairs on their lunch hours (*Budget and time conscious*).

- Manhattan residents who own stylish, luxury watch brands like Tag Heuer, Breitling, or Hamilton looking for expert repairs. (*Luxury watch lovers*).

- USA residents who own vintage Zodiac watches who need expert repairs from a watch shop that they trust. (*Vintage watch lovers, nationwide*).

Similarly, the Las Vegas real estate broker might segment his customers by space need – office, warehouse, retail. Moreover, there might be a segmentation based on those looking to rent vs. buy. And the Miami divorce attorney might segment into men vs. women, those with substantial property vs. those without, those who have children vs. those who do not.

For your second **TODO**, open up your Word document and list customer segments – customers who differ by type (income level, geographic location), by need (high end, low end, rent vs. buy), or even geographic location. Try to see your customers as specific groups with specific needs, rather than one amorphous mega group. Begin to think about how each might search Google differently, using different keywords.

▶▶ Establish Marketing Goals

Moving from business value to customer needs or segments; it's time to think about definable **goals** or **actions** for your website. For most businesses, a good goal is to get a registration / email address / inquiry for a free consult. Our Las Vegas real estate company, for instance, might want visitors to the website to "send a message" about their property needs, or register for a free consult with a leasing specialist. Similarly, our divorce attorney might want a potential client to reach out for a free phone consult, and our watch shop might just want people to call or email to discuss their watch repair needs, and get directions to the shop.

For most businesses, marketing goals on the Web usually boil down to –

- A **registration** – for a free consult, a software download, a free e-book, a newsletter sign up, etc.

- A **sale** – an e-commerce transaction such as the purchase of a candy gift tin on an e-store, or an iPhone skin via PayPal.

A well-constructed website will lead customers to an easy-to-see first step. Here's a screenshot from http://www.reversemortgage.org, one of the top websites for the Google search "reverse mortgage," with the goal clearly marked:

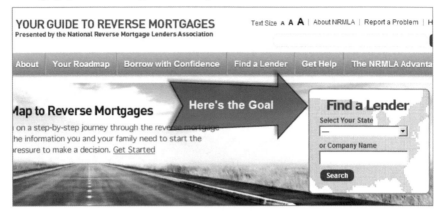

Reversemortgage.org knows what it wants: first, to **rank** at the top of Google search for "reverse mortgage," second, to **get the click**; and third, for a potential customer to start towards the **goal**, i.e. the process of finding a lender (and giving the Website his name, email address, and phone number for a sales follow up!).

Abstractly:

1. Rank high on a Google search query ("reverse mortgage" in this case).

2. Get the click from Google to your website.

3. Once they land, get them to take the "first step" or "goal" (in this case, find a lender).

4. Follow up with them by email or phone to begin the sales process.

Take a moment and look at your web pages from the perspective of a Google searcher. Does it answer a search question? Is the "first step" or "goal" easy to see? Don't make customers think! Don't make customers hunt for goals, or they'll bounce back to Google and be gone.

Defining goals is inseparable from defining your **sales ladder**. Web searchers are actively looking for an answer to their query, and they are anything but passive: if they don't see what they want, click, bounce, bye, and they're gone.

Some marketers talk of a "sales funnel," a concept I do not like because it implies that customers are **passive**, like little marbles that fall into your website and into your registration or sale. I do not think people on the Web (or in life) are passive at all. I think people as **active** searchers, searching Google, clicking to websites, finding what they want (or not), and being quite skeptical about whether they should take the next action.

I like to think of customers not in terms of a "sales funnel" but rather in terms of a "sales ladder." Let me explain.

I think of customers like salmon jumping up from sea level in frigid Alaskan rivers, jumping higher and higher up fish ladders (put there by the Alaskan Department of Fish and Game) to get to their goal: the spawning ground. The fish are motivated (there's breeding to be done), and active participants in the process.

A good Alaskan fishery expert doesn't engineer one **huge, high** jump for the salmon but rather a series of **smaller, easier-to-jump** hurdles that can move the fish from goal one to goal two, etc. Why? Because if the first jump is too high, and too scary, the fish won't make it. Similarly, make your own "first step" non-threatening, and easy!

One of the best early steps in the goal is something **free**.

Having something free (a free webinar, a free consultation, a free e-book) is a tried and true way to make the first step of your ladder easy and non-threatening. People love free, and will give away their email and phone contact information for something useful that is also free. If you are selling something, think of a free sample or money back offer; anything that reduces the risk of making that first buying decision. Using free, make the first step of your sales ladder exciting, enticing, and free!

For your fourth **TODO**, open up your Word document and brainstorm your desired goals (registrations and/or sales) as well as your sales ladder, including the possible use of something "free" to make that first step easy for customers.

For extra credit, begin to think about how you will **measure** these goals. As we will learn in Chapter 6.1, you can use Google Analytics to measure goals such as registrations or sales. But you can also use tactics like special toll-free 800 numbers, vanity phone extensions, and offer codes to track whether someone is coming from a Web search to a phone call into your call center.

Goals and measurability go hand-in-hand.

▶▶ Deliverable: a Goals Worksheet

Now that we've come to the end of Step 1.2, you should have your **DELIVERABLE** ready: a completed **goals worksheet**. This worksheet should define your business value proposition, customer segments, search paths, desired action and sales ladder, and even how you plan to measure customer progress along the search ladder. In Chapter 2.1, we will turn to defining your keywords (which builds upon this knowledge), but first let's turn to the "big picture" of how SEO works.

Basics

I like to think of SEO like a **game**, a competitive game like running a marathon, playing cards, or even **getting a job**. Every game has its rules, of course, and if you don't know the rules of the game, you surely can't win. Now SEO is a subject that has suffered from great confusion, with a blizzard of information and even **dis**information from Google and the SEO industry. But despite this information overload, SEO really isn't that hard to understand.

SEO, to use an analogy, is a lot like the process of getting a job. It has its **resume** (your **website**), its **references** (your inbound **links**), and its job **interview** (your website **landing pages**).

Let's get started!

To Do List:

>> Understand that SEO Parallels Getting a Job

>> Understand "On Page" SEO

>> Understand "Off Page" SEO

>> Set Landing Page Goals

>> Understand that SEO Parallels Getting a Job

Let's consider the search for a job. How does the job search market work? People want to "be found" as the "ideal" candidate for a position. So what do they do? Three important things:

Create a resume. Job seekers create a keyword-heavy resume that explains the job that they want to get, and their qualifications for that job. If, for example, they want a job as a BMW auto mechanic, they create a resume that emphasizes keywords like "auto mechanic," "auto repair," and even "BMW repair" by prominently displaying them in the right places, including the subject line of emails they send out to prospective employers. And employers "scan" resumes looking for those resumes that "match" their keywords.

Cultivate References. Beyond a great resume, the other aspect of job search is cultivating great **references**. Knowing the boss's wife, having the head of the BMW auto mechanic school, or someone else important or influential put in a good word, does what? Gets your resume elevated to the top of the heap, gets it looked at, and possibly gets you the job interview.

Work on Job Interview Skills. Once you get the interview, what's next? The job **interview** is the first step towards landing the job, it's the "free glimpse" of what you have to offer that "sells" the employer on making a financial commitment. Don't blow it at the interview!

Hopefully you can already see that SEO is a lot like getting a job. How so?

Creating a resume equals creating a strong, keyword heavy website. Your website, in a sense, is your business resume, and it needs to have keywords placed on it in strategic places to "talk to" Google as well as human searches, and just as with a job search, you have to research the hot button keywords that people are searching for and place those in strategic position. This is called "**on page**" SEO.

Cultivating references equals going social. Just as you cultivate references to get your resume elevated to the top of the heap, so you cultivate inbound links, fresh buzz, and social mentions to elevate your website to the top of Google search. This is called "**off page** SEO."

Job interview skills equal landing page behavior. Once you get noticed, your next step is a fantastic job interview. The equivalent of the job interview is the **landing behavior** on your website. Once they land from Google, you want them to "take the next step," usually a registration or a sale just as at a job interview, you want them to "take the next step" such as a second interview or a hire

Keep this analogy in the back of your head as you read through the workbook. SEO is a lot like a job search in the following ways:

resume = "on page" SEO

references = "off page" SEO

job interview = "landing page experience"

Can it be that simple? Yes.

Do most people do a bad job of it? Yes.

The fact that most people do a terrible job at something doesn't make it complicated; it just means that the knowledge of how to do it well is relatively rare. Indeed, the fact that most people do SEO badly actually means that it is a <u>huge opportunity</u> for you and your company.

A few simple changes such as placing your keywords into strategic positions on your website can have a huge impact. *You don't have to run faster than the bear, just faster than your buddy!*

Just because most people do it badly doesn't mean you have to!

▶▶ "On Page" SEO

Let's drill down into the first element, "on page" SEO, the equivalent of a great resume. What are the steps? First and foremost, identify your keywords just as you would identify relevant keywords for your resume for the job you wish to get. Then, once you know your keywords, you need to know where to put them.

In terms of "on page" SEO, the main strategic factors are:

Page Tags. Place your keywords strategically in the right page tags, beginning with the TITLE tag on each page, followed by the header tag family, image alt attribute, and HTML cross-links from one page to another on your site.

Keyword Density. Write keyword-heavy copy for your web pages, and pay attention to writing quality. Latent semantic indexing (LSI) means placing your keywords into grammatically correct sentences, and making sure that your writing contains similar and associated words vs. your keyword targets.

Home Page SEO. Use your home page wisely, by placing keywords in strong density on your home page and, again, in natural syntax, and creating "one click" links from your home page to your subordinate pages.

Website structure. Organize your website to be Google friendly, starting with keyword-heavy URLS, cross-linking with keyword text, and using sitemaps and other Google-friendly tactics.

"On page" SEO is all about knowing your keywords and building keyword-heavy content that communicates your priorities to Google just as a good resume communicates your job search priorities to prospective employers. We'll investigate "on page" SEO more deeply in Chapters Two, Three, and Four.

▶▶ "Off Page" SEO

Let's drill down into the second element, "off page" SEO, the equivalent of great references. Here, you do not fully control the elements (unlike in "on page" SEO), so the game is played out in how well you can convince others to talk favorably about you and your website. The main strategic factors of "off page" SEO are as follows:

Link Building. As we shall see, links are the votes of the Web. Getting as many qualified websites to link back to your website, especially high PageRank (high authority) websites using keyword-heavy syntax, is what link building is all about. It's that simple, and that complicated.

Freshness. Like a prospective employer, Google rewards sites that show fresh activity. "What have you done lately?" is a common job interview question, and in SEO you need to communicate to Google that you are active via frequent content updates such as blog posts and press releases.

Social Mentions. Social media is the new buzz of the Internet, and Google looks for mentions of your website on social sites like Google+, Twitter, and Facebook as well as how active your own profiles are.

"Off page" SEO is all about building external links to your site just as getting good references is all about cultivating positive buzz about you as a potential employee. We'll investigate "on page" SEO more deeply in Chapters Four and Five. Oh, and due to the recent Google algorithm change called *Penguin*, we'll emphasize that you want to cultivate *natural* inbound links as opposed to *artificial* links that scream "manipulation" at Google!

▶▶ Set Landing Page Goals

Let's drill down into the third element, "Landing Page Goals," the equivalent of great job interview skills. The point of a great website isn't just to get traffic from Google, after all. It's to move that potential customer up your sales ladder – from website landing to a registration for something free (a "sales lead") or perhaps even a sale.

So in evaluating your website, you want to evaluate each and every page and each and every page element for one variable: do they move customers up the **sales ladder**? Is the desired action (registration or sale) clearly visible on each page, and if so, is it enticing to the customer usually with something free like a free download, free consult, free webinar and the like?

Just as after a job interview, your family and friends ask whether you "got the job," after a Web landing you are asking yourself whether it "got the action" such as a registration or a sale. Web traffic just like sending out resumes is not an end in itself, but a means to an end!

Most of the rest of the SEO Workbook is about doing SEO vs. understanding SEO and the Google algorithm, but check Chapter 7 for "Never stop learning" resources including the primary websites that cover the ever-changing SEO landscape.

Keywords

If Step #1 is "Set the Right Expectations," Step #2 is to define your **keywords**. Your customers start their quest to "find you" by typing in **keywords** or **key phrases** into Google, Yahoo, or Bing. (For simplicity's sake, I'll use the word **keyword** to mean either a single or multi-word phrase as a search engine query). Identifying **customer-centric keywords** is the foundation of effective SEO. Your best keywords match your **business value proposition** with **high volume keywords** used by your customers.

- In **Step 2.1**, we'll brainstorm our list of keywords, focusing on "getting all the words" on paper.

- In **Step 2.2**, we'll turn to organizing these keywords into a structured keyword worksheet.

The **DELIVERABLE** for Step 2.1 is a Microsoft Word document listing all of your possible keywords, called *keyword brainstorm*. For now, don't worry about organization. Your goal is to get **all** your possible keywords on paper, and then in Step 2.2, we'll organize them into a structured **keyword worksheet**.

Let's get started!

TO DO LIST:

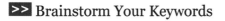 Brainstorm Your Keywords

 Reverse Engineer Competitors' Keywords

>> Use Google Tricks to Identify Possible Keywords

>> Use the AdWords Keyword Planner

>> Deliverable: a Keyword Brainstorm Document

>> Brainstorm Your Keywords

Sit down in a quiet place with a good cup of coffee or tea, or if you prefer a martini, i.e. anything to get your ideas flowing! Brainstorm the keywords by which potential customers might search for you on Google.

Write down each and every potential keyword that comes to mind. You can do this alone, or in a group with your coworkers, friends, or customers. Don't censor yourself because there are no wrong answers.

Begin to "think like a customer" sitting at his or her computer screen at Google:

- **Assume you are a completely new, novice customer.** Assume you know next to nothing. What keywords would you type into Google?

- **Segment your customers into different groups.** What keywords might each group use, and how would they differ from other groups?

- **Are there are any specific "helper" words that a potential customer might use?** Common helper words specify geographic locality (e.g., San Francisco, Berkeley, San Jose), for example. Others specify things like "free," "cheap," "trial," or "information."

For your first **TODO**, open up a Word document, title it "Keyword Brainstorm," and write down each and every possible keyword or keyphrase from your brainstorm session. Get everything on paper. Alternatively, do this as a group exercise and write on a white board. For worksheets to help with this deliverable, use http://bit.ly/keywords-word (Word) | http://bit.ly/keywords-pdf (PDF).

For right now, don't worry about the organization of your keywords. Don't police your thoughts. Write down every word that comes to mind - synonyms, competitor names, misspellings, alternative word orders. Let your mind wander. This is the keyword discovery phase, so be broad!

▶▶ Reverse Engineer Competitors' Keywords

Next, let's do some searches on Google for your target keywords. As you search Google, identify your "Google competitors," that is, companies that are on page one of the Google results and therefore doing well in terms of SEO. You'll want to **reverse engineer** their keywords.

First, click over to their home page or whatever page is showing up on page one of Google for a search that matters to you. Next, view the HTML source. To do this, in Firefox and Chrome, use right click, then **V**iew, **P**age Source. In Internet Explorer, use **V**iew, **S**ource on the file menu. Finally, look for the following tags in the HTML source code:

```
<Title>
<Meta Name="Description" Content="...">
<Meta Name="Keywords" Content="...">
```

For each, write down those keywords your competitor has identified that might also be applicable to you. Here's a screenshot of http://www.globalindustrial.com/c/hvac/fans, one of the top Google performers for the search "industrial fans" with the three critical tags highlighted in yellow -

```
13
14
15
16
17  <!DOCTYPE html PUBLIC "-//W3C//DTD XHTML 1.0 Transitional//EN" "http://ww
18  <html xmlns="http://www.w3.org/1999/xhtml" xml:lang="en" lang="en">
19    <head>
20      <meta http-equiv="Content-Type" content="text/html; charset=iso-8859-
21      <meta http-equiv="Content-Language" content="en-us"/>
22      <title>Pedestal Fans | Agricultural Fans | Blower Fans | Ceiling Fans
23
24      <meta name="category" content="Fans"/>
25
26      <meta name="keywords" content="Fans - Agricultural, Loading Dock, Ped
        Styles & Sizes At Global Industria"/>
27
28      <meta name="description" content="Pedestal Fans - Agricultural Fans,
        From Hundreds Of Styles & Sizes At Global Industrial"/>
29
30
31
32
```

Read each tag out loud. Notice how each tag in the source reveals the "thought process" behind this page, showing the synonyms "fan" for "blower," plus the "types" of fans people might search for - pedestal, agricultural, ceiling, etc. The goal of viewing the source of your competitors pages is to "steal" their keyword ideas, and write down any relevant keywords onto your "keyword brainstorm" document.

VIDEO. Watch a quick video tutorial on how to use "view source" to reverse engineer competitors at http://jm-seo.org/2999-a.

For your second **TODO**, open up your "Keyword Brainstorm" document, and jot down the top five competitors who appear at the top of Google for your target keywords as well as some keyword ideas taken from their TITLE, META DESCRIPTION, and META KEYWORDS tags.

▶▶ Use Google Tricks to Identify Possible Keywords

After you have brainstormed, it's time to use free tools for keyword discovery. You can find a complete list in the companion SEO *Toolbook* (Keywords Chapter), but here are my favorite strategies starting with Google's own free tools.

First, simply go to Google and start typing your keyword. Pay attention to the pull down menu that automatically appears. This is called **Google Suggest** and is based on actual user queries. It's a quick and easy way to find "helper" words for any given search phrase. You can also place a space (hit your space bar) after your target keyword, and then go through the alphabet typing "a", "b", etc.

Here's a screenshot of **Google Suggest** using the key phrase "motorcycle insurance"

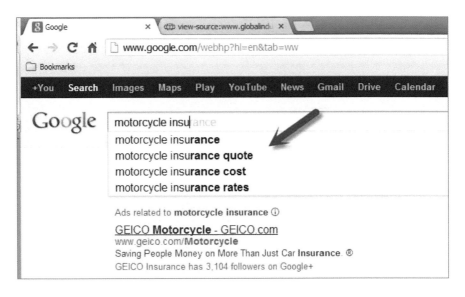

Second, type in one of your target keyword phrases and scroll to the bottom of the Google search page. Google will often give you **related searches** based on what people often search on after their original search. Here's a screen shot for "motorcycle insurance" -

> Searches related to **motorcycle insurance**
>
> motorcycle insurance **rates**   motorcycle insurance **cost**
> **farmers** motorcycle insurance   **average** motorcycle insurance
> **usaa** motorcycle insurance   **state farm** motorcycle insurance
> motorcycle insurance **review**   **how much is** motorcycle insurance

Finally, go back to the top of the Google search box and type the tilde "~" (located at the top left of your keyword) in front of any search term for which they might be synonyms. For example, here is a screenshot of "~lawyer". Synonyms are indicated by Google **bolding** the words on the page.

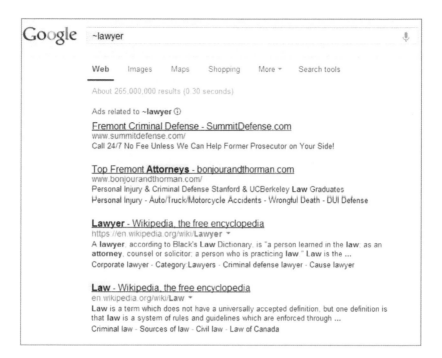

VIDEO. Watch a quick video tutorial on how to use "Google tricks" to generate keyword ideas at http://jm-seo.org/2999-b.

These three Google tricks are great ways to find helper words, related phrases, and synonyms for your target keywords and key phrases. For your third **TODO**, open up your "Keyword Brainstorm" document, and jot down keyword ideas you get from Google Suggest. Pay special attention to helper words!

▶▶ Use the AdWords Keyword Planner

After you have brainstormed and used the Google tricks explained above, you should have a pretty good (albeit messy) list of possible keywords. Now it's time to use Google's most comprehensive keyword tool of them all: Google's own official **AdWords Keyword Planner**. It's free, but you'll need a free AdWords account to use it fully. (You don't have to activate AdWords with any money, but you do need to "sign up" for AdWords to use the tool).

To get to the tool, first sign in to your AdWords account at http://adwords.google.com. Next, go to the "Tools and Analysis" tab in green across the top, and scroll down to "Keyword Planner" or just click on this link: http://jm-seo.org/299-g18. The keyword planner gives you data on keyword search **volume** and **value** if you follow these instructions.

First, on the left hand side where it says "Search for keyword and ad group ideas" type one of your keywords and hit the blue box at the bottom entitled, "Get ideas." Here is a screenshot of the button, which is very easy to miss because it is literally at the bottom of the screen:

This gets you into the tool's real interface. This is where you'll do most of your work, and it looks like this:

Keyword Planner Add ideas to your plan	Your product or service knee pain		
Targeting ?	Ad group ideas	Keyword ideas	
All locations	**Ad group (by relevance)**	**Keywords**	**Avg. monthly searches** ?
All languages			
Google	Keywords like: ...	chronic knee pai...	22,800
Negative keywords	Cause (21)	what causes kn...	7,890

A note to the wise: the new Keyword Planner is not going to go down in Google history as the best-designed user interface! To be blunt, Google has done a pretty terrible job with the user interface but because of Google's search dominance it remains the data source for keyword research. Just be patient, and click around on the tool to learn its operation and secrets.

For purposes of our example, let's assume we are a New York orthopedic surgeon specializing in knee surgery, and so we'll enter "knee pain." After you click "get ideas," you'll see a tab called "Ad group ideas," and one called "keyword ideas." Ignore the "Ad group ideas" (which is pretty worthless)and instead click on "Keyword ideas."

You'll see something like the screenshot below:

Keyword Planner	Your product or service		
Add ideas to your plan	knee pain		

Targeting ?			
United States	Ad group ideas	Keyword ideas	
All languages	Search terms	Avg. monthly searches ?	Competition
Google	knee pain	90,500	High
Negative keywords			

Customize your search ?	Keyword (by relevance)	Avg. monthly searches ?	Competition
Keyword filters			
Avg. monthly searches ≥ 0	knee pain relief	2,400	High

The first thing to understand is what all the columns and pull-outs mean. Starting on the left column, take a look at "Targeting." You'll see here it says "United States." If you click the pencil to the right of "United States," you can drill down to specific states or even cities by typing their names into this space and then clicking "remove" on other entries. This is useful if you'd like to know keyword search volume for specific states; at the city level, the tool isn't very useful as the search volume is often insufficient, however. Alternatively, you can "remove" the United States and target "All locations" which is Googlespeak for the entire world. Note that to activate a change just click elsewhere on the screen or hit enter. (The brilliant engineers at Google failed to clarify how to enter data into the tool!)

Negative keywords also has some utility. You can filter "out" keywords that don't matter to you. For example, if we type in "exercises" it then filters out keyword phrases that contain the word "exercises." Many companies want to filter out words like "free" or "cheap," so use negative keywords for any desired refinement. **Competition** refers to competition on AdWords and organizes that into high, medium, and low; I do not find this a useful data point. **Ad impr share** is only important if you are actually advertising on AdWords.

Refocusing the Keyword Planner. You may notice that the tool gives you very broad matches, so I often recommend that you refocus it to just your target phrase and related phrases. To do that, on the left-hand column where it says Include / Exclude, type the exact same phrase that you are searching into the box at the top ("Only include"). **This paradoxically then *excludes* keyword that do not contain your target phrases.**

In this way, you can zero into just one phrase. Here's a screenshot doing this for our keyword phrase "knee pain" with "knee pain" typed into both the top search box and also the Include / Exclude pull-out as indicated below:

Only include keywords containing the following terms: ?

knee pain|

Exclude keywords containing any of the following terms: ?

Now click on the column "Avg. monthly searches," and the tool will sort your keywords by volume (the number of searches per month for your target geography). Here's a screenshot of this for "knee pain" after having focused the tool by entering "knee pain" in both the top and left include / exclude locations:

Keyword Planner	Your product or service			
Add ideas to your plan	knee pain			

Targeting ?		Ad group ideas	Keyword ideas			⤓
All locations	✎					
All languages	✎	Search terms		Avg. monthly searches ?	Competition ?	Avg. CPC ?
Google	✎	knee pain		165,000	Medium	$1.02
Negative keywords exercises	✎					1 - 1 of
Customize your search ?		Keyword (by relevance)	▼	Avg. monthly searches ?	Competition ?	Avg. CPC ?
Keyword filters	✎					
Avg. monthly searches ≥ 0		pain behind knee		14,800	Low	$0.40
Avg. CPC ≥ $0.00						
Ad impr. share ≥ 0%		knee pain running		8,100	Medium	$0.86

You can see the the average monthly search volume for "knee pain" for "all locations" (i.e., the entire world) is 165,000 searches. The number 1 phrase is "pain behind knee" at 14,800 followed by "knee pain running" at 8,100. **Note that these search volumes refer to exact match only: they take into account only when a searcher enters that phrase and nothing more.** For example, 14,800 people entered "pain behind knee" and no additional words. If you'd like to drill down to a phrase, then you have to re-enter it in both places. Enter "pain behind knee" in both places and Google will give you the related helper words such as "pain behind knee cap," "sharp pain behind knee, etc."

Unfortunately, this new and improved (SIC) version of the tool does **not** yet allow for phrase matching: volumes refer only to exact matches (i.e., those words and no other additional words typed into Google). It has been strongly criticized by the SEO community for this fact because the old Keyword Tool did allow such functionality, but to no avail. So, so far you can only get keyword volumes for exact match. So for now, to compare keyword volumes you are left with manually "guessing" related phrase and entering them into the tool.

You can, however, enter multiple phrases and compare them. Let's take these keywords:

> knee pain
> knee surgery
> knee surgeon
> knee surgeons New York

To compare phrases, enter them as a <u>comma separated phrase</u> as follows and click "Get ideas":

> knee pain, knee surgery, knee surgeon, knee surgeons New York

Here's a screenshot:

This tells us there are 165,000 searches world-wide for "knee pain" (again, exact searches - not phrase match!), 14,800 for "knee surgery," 590 for "knee surgeon" and a very small number for "knee surgeons new york." The CPC column tells us some interesting data about keyword value. The cost that advertisers are willing to pay per click starts at $1.02 for "knee pain," then to $1.92 for "knee surgery" and up to $2.39 for "knee surgeon." This is a hint that the keyword value of the latter term is worth more because someone who enters "knee pain" might be looking for a Tylenol, while someone entering "knee surgery" or even better "knee surgeon" is very close to engaging a surgeon for a very expensive operation. The tool clues us into the difference between early-stage, "educational" keywords and late-stage "transactional" keywords.

In sum, you can use the "Avg. CPC" column as a clue as to what your competitors are bidding on keywords, and therefore a way to identify which keywords are closer to a user action such as a registration or sale.

That said, you still need to rely on your instinct to determine your best keywords and then bolster that with real data from your Google Analytics, which we discuss in the last chapter. The Keyword Planner is only a tool, and the art of SEO still means a lot of head-scratching to identify those keywords that are not just high volume but also high value. Riches, my friend, are in the niches.

> **VIDEO.** Watch a quick video tutorial on how to use the Google Keyword Planner to generate keyword ideas at http:// jm-seo.org/2999-w

For your final **TODO**, open up your "Keyword Brainstorm" document, and jot down keyword volumes and the CPC values of relevant keywords. Again, don't worry about being organized. Just get the rough ideas down on paper.

▶▶ Deliverable: a Keyword Brainstorm Document

Now we've come to the end of Step 2.1, and you should have the chapter **DELIVERABLE** ready: your "Keyword Brainstorm" document.

Remember the "Keyword Brainstorm" document will be messy. Its purpose is to get all relevant keywords, competitors, and keyword ideas down on paper. In Step 2.2, we will turn to **organizing** our keywords into a structured **keyword worksheet**.

2.2

Keyword Worksheet

Now that you have a keyword **brainstorm document**, it's time to get organized! Step #2.2 is all about taking the disorganized list of keywords and organizing them into a structured Excel worksheet that reflects keyword volume, value, and search patterns. You'll use your keyword worksheet as your "SEO blueprint" for many tasks, such as measuring your rank on Google, structuring your website to tell Google what keywords matter to you, to write better blog posts and so on.

The **DELIVERABLES** for Step 2.2 are a Microsoft Excel **keyword worksheet**, and a **rank measurement / baseline** of where your websites stands for target keywords searches on Google.

Let's get Started!

TO DO LIST:

>> Create Your Keyword Worksheet

>> Deliverable: Your Keyword Worksheet

>> Measure Your Google Rank vs. Keywords

>> Deliverable: Rank Measurements on Your Keyword Worksheet

>> Create Your Keyword Worksheet

After you complete your **keyword brainstorm** document, you may be amazed at how many possible keywords or key phrases a customer might type into Google! If you look deeper, however, you'll realize that keywords follow logical patterns. These keyword groups are the foundational building blocks of good SEO. The first step towards building an effective **keyword worksheet** is to begin to organize keywords into groups.

For your first **TODO**, open up an Excel spreadsheet, call it "Keyword Worksheet." You can download a sample keyword worksheet at http://bit.ly/sample-keyword. In your own Excel spreadsheet, create columns for the following:

Core Keywords. These are the minimum words necessary to create a relevant search. If you are a medical malpractice attorney, for example, then "medical malpractice" is a core keyword, as are "hospital malpractice" and "medical negligence."

Helper Keywords. Common helpers are geographic like San Francisco, Berkeley, Oakland. Or terms like "lawyer" or "attorney."

Representative Search Queries. Take your core keywords plus your helpers and build out some "real" search queries that potential customers might use. Group these by keyword family.

Search Volumes. Indicate the volume of searches (where available) as obtained from the primary Google keyword tool.

Search Value. Indicate whether a given keyword family is of high, low, or negative value to you and your business. Does it indicate a searcher who is probably a target customer? If your answer is strongly yes, then this is a "high value" search term! Does it clearly indicate a non-customer? If so, this is a "low value" or even a "negative" search term.

Competitors. As you do your searches, write down the URL's of competitors that you see come up in your Google searches. These will be useful as mentors that you can emulate as you build out your SEO strategy.

Negative Keywords. Are there any keywords that indicate someone is definitely not your customer? These negative keywords are not so important for SEO, but if you engage in AdWords, they will become very useful.

Volume vs. Value. Let's review for a moment the trade-off between keyword **volume** and keyword **value**, focusing on educational vs. transactional keywords. Educational keywords tend to be higher volume but lower value, while transactional keywords tend to be lower volume but higher value.

To use an example, consider "knee pain." Many people search for "knee pain," looking to understand what causes knee pain and what are the available remedies. A few people will search in the middle ground for "knee surgery," when they are considering possibly getting an artificial knee. And just a very few will search for "knee surgeon" or even more focused, "best knee surgeon in San Francisco."

For a knee surgeon in San Francisco, however, the highest value searches are those on the right – the transactional searches "knee surgeons in San Francisco" vs. the higher volume searches "knee pain" or even "knee surgery."

Here's a screenshot from the Google Keyword Tool (http://jm-seo. org/299-g18) of these searches, showing the volume and value trade-off:

Notice that there are many more searches for "knee pain" (246,000 in the USA last month) vs. for "knee surgeon" (2,900) but that the cpc (cost-per-click) is much, much higher for "knee surgeon" ($4.11 vs. $1.90). This is because AdWords advertisers have figured out that the "knee surgeon" search is more likely to end in a high value, paying patient while the "knee pain" search has a lot of people who are only going to buy an aspirin.

Use this logic for your own keyword targeting in SEO. It's not just **volume** or **value** when you structure your keywords: it's volume *and* value. As they say "riches are in the niches," so you are looking to rank well on keyword searches that are a "sweet spot" for you, where relatively high volume keywords hit high value to you (searches that are likely to end in a sale or sales lead). The good news is that it is actually easier to dominate the more focused, higher value transactional searches, generally speaking.

Search Patterns. Next, let's review structural patterns. It is very important to conceptualize the way that people search, i.e., the mindsets by which they approach your information. Let's take the example of Ron Gordon Watch Repair (http://www.rongordon-watches.com). This business repairs luxury watches in New York City. What are the basic structural search patterns?

> **Watch Repair.** These are searches built around the most basic search: "watch repair" and in some cases with the added helper geographic words of "NYC," "New York, NY" or "Manhattan." These are the more educational, less focused searches.

> **Brand Searches.** These are searches by people who have a specific brand, e.g., Breitling. Their searches are much more focused such as "Breitling Repair NYC."

> **Vintage Searches.** Ron Gordon has a nice business in vintage watch repair, and the sale of vintage Zodiac watches, so these searches reflect people who are interested in vintage Zodiac watches and/or their repair.

> **Esoteric Searches.** These are very focused searches such as "Watch repair near Grand Central Station" or "How to tell if a ROLEX is fake?"

In sum, the keyword worksheet for Ron Gordon Watches should reflect keyword volume, value (as measured by the "fit" between the keyword search and what Ron Gordon Watches has to offer), and the structural search patterns that reflect the "mindset" by which people search.

VIDEO. Watch a quick video tutorial on building a keyword worksheet at http://jm-seo.org/2999-d.

▶▶ Deliverable: Your Keyword Worksheet

After some brainstorming, hard work, and organization, you should have your first **DELIVERABLE** ready: a **keyword worksheet** in an Excel spreadsheet. The first tab should be a high level overview to relevant keywords, reflecting the structural search patterns that generate the **keyword groups**, next the keyword volumes as measured by the Google keyword tool, and finally the values measured by the Google cost-per-click data and your own judgment as to which search queries are most likely to lead to a sale or sales lead.

Your keyword worksheet is your blueprint for successful SEO, but don't think of it as a static document! Rather, think of your keyword worksheet as an evolving "work in progress." There is as much art as science in SEO, and in many cases, the formal tools like the Google keyword tool only get you so far.

Gut instinct as to how your customers search, especially which searches are likely to be close to a sale, can be just as valuable as numeric research.

▶▶ Measure Your Google Rank vs. Keywords

Now that you have built out your **keyword worksheet**, your next **TODO**, is to measure your **rank** on target Google searches. Google rank, of course, refers to where your website is on the first page Google returns for a search queries. Counting the organic results only, there are positions 1, 2, and 3 (the "Olympic" positions) and then positions four through ten ("page one" positions). Anything beyond position ten is not good.

Why do we care about our Google rank? First of all, the Olympic positions (1, 2, and 3) capture the lion's share of clicks; by many estimates, over 60%! Second, being on page one means you are at least "in the game." But third, as good SEO experts, we want to measure our rank before, during and after our SEO efforts to measure our progress and return on investment (ROI). We can also feed this data back into our strategy so that we can then focus our content and link efforts (e.g. blog posts, product pages, press releases, link building) on searches where we are beyond page one vs. creating new content for searches for which we are already in top positions.

Fortunately, there are two great tools for measuring your Google rank, both of which are free. The first tool can be found at http://bit.ly/sitemap-rank . Simply type your domain in, enter your target keyword, and hit search. This tool is a great eye-saver!

Here's a screenshot for rongordonwatches.com for the search "Rolex Watch Repair NYC":

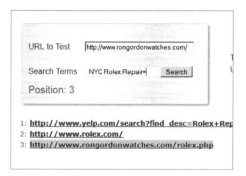

The second recommended free tool is called "Rank Checker" and can be downloaded from http://bit.ly/seo-book-rank. It is available only for Firefox.

Rank Checker
The most popular rank checking application on the web.

Once the tool is downloaded and installed as a Firefox plugin, enter your keyword list in the tool as follows. In the file menu, select Tool > Rank Checker > Run. Then click "Add Multiple" keywords. Enter your target keywords plus your domain. In the "Options" tab (Tool, Rank Checker, Options), be sure to check "Don't use Google Personalized Results" and set "Delay between Queries" to 5 seconds to analyze ten words or less; to 99 seconds if you are going to run a very long list

Here's a screenshot showing how to get to the Rank Checker tool via the Firefox menu:

Use the resulting report to identify "strengths" (places where you appear in the top three or top ten) and "weaknesses" (keywords for which you appear beyond page one, or not at all). Having identified your keyword rank weaknesses, you now know where to target your SEO efforts. Blog, build links, issue news - do whatever it takes to elevate your standing for your "weak" keywords!

The free "Rank Checker" tool also gives you more than just a "snapshot" of your Google rank. You can systematically create and save rank reports by keyword, compare yourself to competitors, and export these reports to Excel. In this way, you can chart your absolute rank on Google for your target keywords over time, plus compare / contrast yourself with competitors. All automatically!

> **VIDEO.** Watch a quick video tutorial on measuring keyword rank at http://jm-seo.org/2999-e.

As you check rank, be sensitive to the fact that the free tools generally measure only your organic rank. If local search is important to you, you need to manually check your rank on Google+ local. Similarly if video SEO or press release SEO matter, you'll need to check those ranks manually as well. There are unfortunately no really good free tools for measuring blended search results on Google.

▶▶ Deliverable: Rank Measurements on Your Keyword Worksheet

The **DELIVERABLE** for rank of course is to copy / paste the rank metrics into the **keyword worksheet** and note the date of rank measurement. I usually create tabs in the spreadsheet and paste ten to fifty sample keyword phrases. It's a best practice to measure your rank at least monthly.

Page Tags

Once you know your keywords via Step #2, where do you put them? "Page Tag" SEO is the quick and easy answer to that question, and it is the most important aspect of Step #3. In Step #3, you take your keywords from your keyword worksheet, place them in strategic locations on individual web pages via page tags, restructure your website to send clear signals to Google about your keyword targets, and finally conduct a website audit to identify necessary tag and structural changes.

Let's get Started!

TO DO LIST:

>> Understand Page Tags and SEO

>> Weave Keywords into Page Tags

>> Deliverable: an Individual Page Tag Audit

>> Leverage Keyword Density for SEO

>> Set up Your Home Page

>> Deliverable: Home Page Page Tag Audit

>> Understand Page Tags and SEO

HTML is the language of the Web, and it is based on what are called "tags" in HTML. At a very simple level, if you want a word to appear bold, you might put the "tag" **<strong>** around the word such as *"We sell **<strong>**running shoes**</strong>**"* in the HTML text of the web page. This will display in browsers as:

We sell **running shoes**.

If you are using an WYSIWYG editor like WordPress or Dreamweaver, the editor may do this for you, but behind the scenes the true foundation of the Web is HTML, and the foundation of HTML is **page tags**.

To see the true HTML behind the visible Web, go to any webpage with your browser, right click, "View Source" in Firefox, Internet Explorer, or Chrome. The HTML code you see is the true language of the Web, and this code is what Google or Bing actually uses to index a web page. For example, here is a screenshot of the HTML source code for Geico's page on "Motorcycle Insurance" with the open and close tags highlighted in yellow for the META DESCRIPTION tag and the TITLE tag, which are both very important tags for SEO:

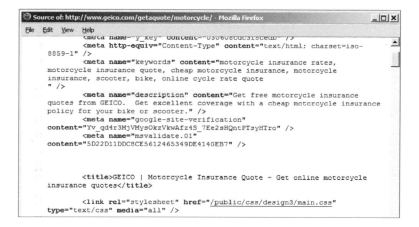

What most people don't realize is that page tags not only structure how a website looks in a browser. **Page tags also send powerful messages to Google about what a web page is about!** In a very simple way, if your page has <**strong**>running shoes</strong> on it, you are not just bolding the word *running* shoes in the browser; you are also signaling Google that the keyword phrase *running shoes* is important to you!

PAGE TAGS SIGNAL
KEYWORD PRIORITIES
TO GOOGLE

All the tags, of course, are not equal! To understand this, let's use an analogy: **page tags are like the cards in poker**. Now everybody knows that the *Ace* is more powerful than the *King*, and the *King* more powerful than the *Deuce*. These are the "rules of poker." What most people do not realize on the Web is that there are rules to SEO success as well, starting with the value of the page tags.

Each tag communicates to the Google algorithm a different keyword weight, just as each card in a game of poker has a different value!

To succeed at poker, you have to understand that the Ace is worth more than the deuce; to succeed at SEO you have to understand that the <TITLE> tag is much more powerful than the <BOLD> tag, and so on and so forth!

Here is a breakdown showing the most important page tags "as if" you were playing a game of poker with Google and your competitors:

<TITLE> = Ace
Most important tag on any page, place your target keyword in the <TITLE> tag of each page. <TITLE> of the home page is the most powerful tag on any website. (66 visible characters; 80 indexed).

<A HREF> = King
Keyword-heavy links cross reference pages to each other, and communicate keywords to Google.

<IMG ALT> = Queen
Have at least one image per page, and put your target keyword into the ALT attribute of the image.

<H1> = Jack
Google loves the header family, so use at least one <H1> per page. Use <H2>, <H3> sparingly.

<META DESCRIPTION > = 10
If you include the target keyword in the <META DESCRIP-TION> tag, Google will use it 90% of the time. (155 character limit).

<BODY> or keyword density = 9
Write keyword-heavy prose on each and every page of the website. Aim for natural syntax and about 5% keyword density.

<STRONG>, <B>, <EM> = 3, 4, 5
Use bold and italicize keywords on the page, strategically.

<META KEYWORDS> = Joker
Ignored by Google. Use it as a "note to self" about the keyword targets for a particular page.

Google produces a very good official guide to SEO that emphasizes just how important tag structure is to Google and SEO. I strongly recommend that you download the guide and read it thoroughly at http://bit.ly/google-seo-starter.

VIDEO. Watch a video tutorial of the major page tags for SEO at http://jm-seo.org/2999-h.

The end result of page tags is to understand that page tags communicate your keywords to Google, so your first **TODO** is pretty obvious: weave your keywords into your page tags, starting with the all-important TITLE tag.

▶▶ Weave Keywords into Page Tags

Now that you know that the TITLE tag is the most important tag, that Google likes the header tag family, and that each web page should have at least one image tag with the ALT attribute defined to include a keyword, you are ready to write a strong SEO page or re-write an existing page to better communicate keyword priorities to Google.

Here's how:

1. Define your target keywords. Using your keyword work-sheet as well as the various keyword tools, define your target keywords. A best practice is to focus on a single keyword per individual product page or blog post.

2. Write a keyword-heavy TITLE tag. The TITLE tag should be less than 80 characters, with the most important keywords on the left.

3. Write a keyword-heavy META DESCRIPTION tag. The META DESCRIPTION tag has a 90% chance of being the visible description on Google, so write one that includes your keywords but is also pithy and exciting. Its job is to "get the click" from Google.

4. Write a few keyword-heavy header tags. Start with an H1 tag and throw in a couple of H2 tags around keyword phrases.

5. Include at least one image with the ALT attribute defined. Google likes to see at least one image on a page, with the keywords around the ALT attribute.

6. Cross-link via keyword phrases. Embed your target keyword phrases in links that link your most important pages across your website.

7. Write keyword dense text. Beyond just page tags, Google looks to see a good keyword density (about 3-5%) and keywords used in natural English syntax following good grammar.

A good way to learn how to write a strong SEO page is to do a "page autopsy."

VIDEO. Watch a quick video tutorial of a page autopsy at http://jm-seo.org/2999-f.

DON'T OVERDO IT!

Finally, don't *overdo* it! We live in a post-*Penguin*, post-*Panda* world (two recent Google algorithm updates that cracked down on "overoptimization" by overly aggressive SEO experts). If you *underdo* your page tags vs. keywords, your website doesn't talk to Google. If you *overdo* it, stuffing too many keywords, Google can penalize you. Find the middle ground characterized by the winners in your industry and be as text heavy and dense as they are, but

not aggressively more so.

▶▶ Deliverable: an Individual Page Tag Audit

The first **DELIVERABLE** for Step Three is a page tag audit. Take an existing page of your website, and compare it against the desired target keyword. Using the worksheet provided, audit the page for how well it communicates the priority keywords to Google. A nifty tool to use on this audit is the Metamend Keyword Density tool at http://jm-seo.org/299-w1 and another really good free tool is by SEO Workers at http://jm-seo.org/299-w2.

Here's a screenshot of the Geico Motorcycle Insurance Page (http://www.geico.com/getaquote/motorcycle) in the Metamend tool:

Input your own web page into the tool and check the visual tag cloud. Hover over keywords to check density and position. The page's target keywords should be clearly and prominently indicated in the tool; if not, you are not correctly signaling keyword priorities to Google! Try the same exercise with the SEO Workers tool.

> **WORKSHEETS.** For your **DELIVERABLE**, analyze your website's existing Page Tag vs. target keyword status, and devise a "quick fix" strategy for an individual web page to improve keyword placement in important tags. Use the worksheet at http://bit.ly/pt-doc (Word) | http://bit.ly/pt-pdf (PDF) to audit keywords vs. page tags for individual pages.

▶▶ Leverage Keyword Density for SEO

As you are writing new pages or analyzing existing ones, keep in mind that **keyword density** on the Web is much, much more **redundant** than in normal English writing.

Few SEO experts and even fewer average marketers really realize just how *redundant, repetitious, repeating, reinforcing,* and *reiterating* strong prose is for Google! Furthermore, it's not just about stringing keywords in comma, comma, comma phrases. The Google algorithm clearly analyzes text and looks for natural syntax, so be sure to write in complete sentences following the rules of grammar and spelling. (This is especially true after the so-called "Panda Update" to the Google algorithm).

So, write keyword heavy text in natural English syntax sentence, while avoiding comma, comma, comma phrases. There is no simple answer here: you have to not overdo it, but not underdo it, either. Keyword density needs to be the Goldilocks setting of "just right."

What keyword density is "just right?"

Here's a screenshot of the Geico motorcycle insurance page, using CTRL+F in Firefox to highlight the occurrences of the word "motorcycle":

Let's Ride® – Get Your Motor Running and Get a
Motorcycle Insurance Quote.

Rev up your savings with motorcycle insurance from GEICO. No matter what
you own – a sport bike, cruiser, standard, touring bike, or a sweet custom ride,
you can turn to us for great rates and great coverage. We even offer scooter
insurance. Enjoy the freedom of the open road knowing that the Gecko®'s got
your back! Let's Ride®

Get free motorcycle insurance quotes anytime.

Why Choose GEICO for Motorcycle Insurance?

Thought that GEICO was all about car insurance, did you? Think again! We
take motorcycles as seriously as you do, and we're pleased to provide you with
top-quality coverage for your bike. With GEICO, you get:

> Outstanding customer service (rated 4.7 out of 5 by our motorcycle insurance

How keyword dense is a page? I call this the "pink and pinch test". Find pages for very competitive Google searches (such as "motorcycle insurance" or "reverse mortgage" or "online coupons"), highlight their keywords by using CTRL+F in Firefox, read the text aloud and pinch yourself every time the keyword is used. At the end of the page, you should be in pain! If you are not in pain, the density is too low. If you're in the hospital, it's too high. In terms of metrics, a good rule of thumb is 3-5 % density, but remember also that it's not just numeric density but the occurrence of keywords in normal sentences that matter.

EYE CANDY AT TOP
TEXT AT BOTTOM

There is a trade-off between the heavy, redundant text favored by Google and the clean, iPhone like picture websites favored by humans. The usual solution is to put the eye candy for humans towards the top, and the stuff for Google towards the bottom. Revisit many of the pages on Geico.com or Progressive.com and you'll notice how the eye candy for humans is at the top, and the redundant text for Google is at the bottom.

>> Set up Your Home Page

Your home page is your "front door" to Google and the **most important page** of your website. Google rewards beefy, keyword-heavy home pages that have a lot of text. Think carefully about every word that occurs on this page, and about the way each word is "structured" by embedding it into good HTML page tags. Here are your important "to do's" for your home page:

- **Identify your customer-centric, top three keywords.** These three "most important" words must go into your home page <TITLE> tag, the most powerful tag on your website!

- **Repeat the <TITLE> tag content in the <H1> tag on the page.** There should be at least one <H1> but no more than three per page.

- **Identify your company's major product / service offerings.** Re-write these using customer centric keywords, and have <H2> tags leading to these major landing pages, nested inside of <A HREF> tags. Be sure to include the keywords inside the <H2> and <A HREF> tags!

- **Have Supporting Images.** Google rewards pages that have images with ALT attributes that are keyword heavy. Don't overdo this, but have at least one and no more than about seven images on your home page that have keywords in their ALT attributes.

- **Create keyword-focused one click links.** Link down from your home page to defined landing pages around target keyword phrases.

- **Write lengthy, keyword-rich content for your home page.** You need not just structural elements, but lots of beefy prose on your home page that clarifies to Google what your company is "about."

For good home page ideas, look at Progressive (http://www.progressive.com), as well as some of SEO-savvy Bay Area medical malpractice attorneys such as http://www.walkuplawoffice.com and http://www.maryalexanderlaw.com. Another good one is http://www.sfflowershop.com. Scroll to the bottom and notice all the keyword heavy text "buried" for Google to find! View their HTML source and look at how they weave their keywords into strategic tags.

VIDEO. Watch a quick video tutorial on effective SEO home pages at http://jm-seo.org/2999-g.

▶▶ Deliverable: Home Page Page Tag Audit

In the next chapter, we'll learn a bit more about how website structure influences Google and SEO, but we can begin the process now by doing a page tag audit for your home page. The most powerful tag on your website is the home page TITLE tag, so start there. Drill down to the text content on your home page and verify that it contains the priority keyword targets identified in your keyword worksheet. Copy / paste your existing home page URL into the SEO Workers free tool (http://jm-seo.org/299-w2)

and compare / contrast: is your home page "telling Google" your priority keywords?

WORKSHEETS. For your **DELIVERABLE**, analyze your home page's existing Page Tag vs. target keyword status, and devise a "quick fix" strategy to improve keyword placement in important tags. Use the free worksheets for your home page at PDF: http://bit.ly/hpg-pdf | Word: http://bit.ly/hpg-doc.

Website Structure

Website structure - the "organization" of your website - is a major part of **Step #3**. Whereas in **page tags** you approach SEO from the perspective of individual web pages, in website structure you should turn your attention to how your *entire* website communicates keyword priorities to Google. How you name your files, how you "reach out" to Google, and how you optimize your landing pages all combine to make a *good* SEO strategy, *great*!

Let's get Started!

TO DO LIST:

>> Define SEO Landing Pages

>> Deliverable: a Landing Page Inventory

>> Use Keyword Heavy URLs over Parameter URLs

>> Leverage the Home Page for One Click Links

>> Deliverable: a Website Structure Audit

>> Create Google Friendly Files

>> Deliverable: Google Friendly Files Checklist

>> Define SEO Landing Pages

In SEO, a **landing page** is a page you create that targets very **specific keyword phrases**. For most companies, your landing pages will reflect your product or service offerings, adjusted for how "real customers" search for them on Google. Companies in competitive industries like insurance, law, online coupon shopping and other industries where the SEO competition is fierce all use landing pages to help get to the top of Google!

Landing pages, however, are not simply about "page tags." Rather, they are always "one click" from the home page, thereby leveraging the home page's SEO power to focus Google's attention on these highly valuable keywords. Behind the scenes, there are also link-building efforts for most successful landing pages.

As an example, let's take a look at http://www.progressive.com. Notice how the major product offerings are "one click" from the home page, and how the link structure reflects the target keywords. Here's a screenshot with the landing pages highlighted in yellow.

Notice how each landing page mirrors a logical keyword target (not just "auto" but "auto insurance," not just "homeowners" but "homeowners insurance"), and is "one click" down from the home page. By "one click," we mean just that: go to the home page, and simply click once on these links: you then land on the defined landing page. Google, in turn, interprets these "one click" links as a major signal of a keyword's importance.

Next, click down to a specific page, such as the "motorcycle" page and notice how it is keenly SEO optimized for the target phrase "motorcycle insurance" plus helper words like "quote." You can see this clearly from its TITLE tag which is:

```
<title>Motorcycle Insurance: Motorcycle Insur-
ance Quotes - Progressive</title>
```

For most websites, a good rule of thumb is to identify three to ten priority landing pages, which will each be laser focused on a single target keyword phrase and be "one click" from the home page.

If your business has a local element, it is often useful to create localized landing pages for individual cities or towns that are "helper words" for your keywords. For example, Stamford Uniform and Linen (http://www.stamfordlinen.com) wants to dominate Google not only for keyword phrases such as "Stamford Linen Service" (where the business is located) but for those in

nearby towns, such as "Hartsdale Linen Service" or "Greenwich CT Linen Service." One method to accomplish this is localized landing pages.

Check out the company's home page, scroll to the bottom and notice the "one click" links to landing pages for target cities plus the keyword search "uniform rental service." For example, the Hartsdale page at http://www.stamfordlinen.com/Hartsdale.html. Also notice how each landing page is unique, with content at the bottom of each city that is unique and different from the others in the set. Try some Google searches such as "Stamford Linen Service," "Hartsdale Linen Service," or "Greenwich CT Linen Service" to see how effective localized landing pages can be!

> **VIDEO.** Watch a video tutorial on SEO landing pages at http://jm-seo.org/2999-i.

However, be **careful** in constructing too many of these localized landing pages! Technically, Google considers these "doorway pages" and a "violation" of its "terms of service." Don't overdo it!

Here is one of the trade-offs of SEO: if you are too *aggressive*, you'll anger Google. But if you are too passive, you'll never get to the top. You can read all the Google rules at http://bit.ly/google-rules but just remember: Google writes the rules to frighten people from doing anything (other than advertising on AdWords).

Find your sweet spot between the two extremes.

▶▶ Deliverable: a Landing Page Inventory

A major DELIVERABLE for Step Three, therefore, is an inventory of your landing pages, namely all that should exist, to reflect your major keyword patterns as described in your keyword worksheet. Using the worksheets below in combination with your keyword worksheet, create a list of your high priority landing pages. Each page will then be optimized via page tags and ultimately "one click" from the home page, using a keyword heavy syntax.

WORKSHEETS. For your DELIVERABLE, create a list of your existing (and desired) landing pages. Then draft out required page tag and content changes necessary to bring the pages up to par. Use the free worksheets at http://bit.ly/structure-pdf (PDF) and http://bit.ly/structure-doc (Word).

▶▶ Use Keyword Heavy URLs over Parameter URLs

URLs or web addresses are what you see in the URL bar at the top of the browser. Google pays a lot of attention to URLs; URLs that contain target keywords clearly help pages climb to the top of Google.

How do we know that? Try a few competitive Google searches such as "Reverse Mortgage Calculator" and look how the URLs that are on page one often contain the target keywords. Here's a screenshot of a few of the websites on page one of Google for that search, with the URLS that contain keywords highlighted in yellow:

What's the take-away? If possible, choose a domain that contains your target keywords. Beyond that, make sure that your URLs (file names) contain the target keywords.

Consider these two examples:

> **Example 1 / Geek File Name** - *http://www.yourcompany. com/files/ llk1/2/kyoklaol.html.* No "clues" to Google as to what is "contained" inside these directories and files.

> **Example 2 / English File Name** - *http://www.sf-attorney. com/medical-malpractice/obstetrics.html.* The domain, directories, and file names all indicate that this is a medical malpractice attorney, specializing in suing OB/GYN doctors.

By the way, what goes for URLs also goes for images: name your images after keywords just as you name your URLs after keywords. Rather than naming an image "image215.jpg" have your graphic designer name your images after your keywords such as "medical-malpractice.jpg."

As part of the **DELIVERABLE** for Step #3, conduct an inventory of your website URLs and graphic file names. Are they keyword heavy? Do the visible keywords match the keyword themes from your keyword worksheet?

Just as important, **avoid parameter URLs.** Parameter URLs are URLs that contain numeric, crazy, geeky codes such as the question mark (?), percent sign (%), equals sign (=), or SessionIDs (often marked SESSID=), these indicate to Google that these are "temporary" pages not worth indexing. Static, keyword heavy URL's far outperform URLs that tell Google a website is database-driven via geeky parameter URLs.

PARAMETER URLS = KISS OF (SEO) DEATH

Here's an example URL from http://www.on24.com, a leading web event company but one with absolutely terrible URLs from an SEO perspective:

> https://event.on24.com/eventRegistration/EventLobbyServlet?
> target=registration.jsp&eventid=596868&*sessionid=1&key*=
> 454CA2FBB6E884C771E293C18049F75E&*partnerref*=0
> sm&
> sourcepage=register

To Google, that looks like a "here today, gone tomorrow" URL that is not worth indexing! **Avoid parameter URLs at all costs as they are the kiss of (SEO) death! Google severely deprecates them in its search results!**

If you do have parameter based URLs, **insist** that your webmaster convert them to "pseudo static" URLs. You can Google "pseudo static" URLs for articles on this topic.

▶▶ Leverage the Home Page for One Click Links

Google interprets your home page as the most powerful page on your website, and as we saw in the Page Tags chapter, you want to have lots of keyword-heavy text on the home page. In addition, you should embed our most important keywords into the home page TITLE tag. Beyond that, you should leverage your home page as a "one click" gateway to your landing pages. It's as if your HTML communicated this message to Google:

```
Home Page > One Click to Landing Pages = Hey
Google! These keywords are important to us!
```

Google also looks at the directory structure, namely the presence of keywords in URLs and how "far" those URLs are from the home page or "root" directory. So, in addition to naming your directories and files after your keyword families and high priority keywords, and placing "one click" links from your home page, create a directory structure that is "**shallow**" or "**flat**."

http://www.yourcompany.com/medical-malpractice /sue-doctors.html (2nd level)

is seen by Google as "more important" than

http://www.yourcompany.com/1/files/new/medical-malpractice/sue-doctors.html (5th level)

Thirdly, your home page needs to communicate "freshness" to Google by having at least three *fresh* press releases and/or three new blog posts. Having new, fresh content that is "one click" from the home page signals to Google that your website is alive and updated (vs. a stagnant site that might be out of business), so it's a best practice to rotate press releases and/or blog posts through the home page as "one click" links.

VIDEO. Watch a video tutorial on SEO-friendly home pages at http://jm-seo.org/2999-g.

WORKSHEETS. For your **DELIVERABLE**, inventory your home page for SEO. Use the free worksheets at http://bit.ly/hpg-pdf (PDF) and http://bit.ly/hpg-doc (Word).

▶▶ Deliverable: a Website Structure Audit

At this point, you have the major components of the chapter **DELIVERABLE**: a **website audit**. Using the worksheets, outline:

1. **Your target landing pages.** These are your product or service pages that match common keywords searches your customers do on Google. Inventory the ones that you have as well as the ones that you need to create, and then outline the SEO-friendly content you will write (or rewrite) and weave into the correct tag structure.

2. **Your home page.** Leverage your home page as a "one click" gateway down to your target keywords, including using your home page to send "freshness signals" to Google with "one click" links to at least three timely press releases and/or blog posts.

3. **Your URL structure.** Avoid parameter (numeric, special character) based URLs in favor of keyword heavy URLs, and build a "shallow" website organization.

▶▶ Create Google Friendly Files

Google rewards websites that make its job easier! Set up sitemaps for Google (and Bing), and participate in their official programs for Webmasters. First, create an **HTML site map** that makes it easy for a search engine spider to go from Page 1 to Page 2 to Page 3 of your website. If you use Javascript / CSS pull downs for navigation, your HTML site map is a critical alternative path for Google to index your website. Second, the free tool at (http:// bit.ly/go-webtools) to create your XML site map. Third, create a robots.txt file that points to your XML sitemap.

Fourth, after you have created these files, log on to Google's Webmaster Tools (http://bit.ly/uYnvTq) and create your **free account** if you haven't done so already. Then submit your **sitemap.xml** file to Google. Pay attention as well to your "crawl errors" and "HTML suggestions." All things being equal, sites that participate in Webmaster tools will beat out sites that do not.

Here's a screen shot of how to submit an XML sitemap via Google webmaster tools:

>> Deliverable: Google Friendly Files Checklist

Your **DELIVERABLE** at this point is whether you have created the following Google-friendly files, and signed up for Google webmaster tools:

1. **Is there a robots.txt file?** Type in your website domain plus robots.txt. You should see a robots.txt file, and it should indicate the location of your XML sitemap. (For example: http://www.jm-seo.org/robots.txt).

2. **Is there an XML sitemap?** The robots.txt file should point to its location, with the best practice being to place it at http://www.jm-seo.org/sitemap.xml.

3. **Is there an HTML sitemap?** This should be "one click" from the home page, and every page on the website should be "one click" from your HTML sitemap.

Finally, you should have joined (and verified) Google webmaster tools for your website (http://bit.ly/uYnvTq) as well as Bing Webmaster tools (http://jm-seo.org/299-w3).

SEO Audit

SEO, like physical fitness, is all about results. It doesn't matter how much you "know" about physical fitness if you don't "do" anything about it! Similarly, in SEO, it doesn't matter how much you "know" about SEO if you don't "do" SEO! So before we turn to tactics such as content marketing and "off page" SEO, let's review what we've learned so far, and start doing SEO by conducting an "on page" SEO audit. (Remember that "on page" SEO has to do only with your website vs. "off page" SEO which concerns inbound links, social mentions, and freshness).

Let's get Started!

TO DO LIST:

>> Deliverable: a Keyword Audit

>> Deliverable: a Page Tag Audit

>> Deliverable: a Home Page Audit

>> Deliverable: a Website Structure Audit

>> Deliverable: a Keyword Audit

SEO, as we have learned, begins with keywords. Do you know your keywords? Do you really know your keywords? Companies that really know their keywords for SEO understand:

- **Keyword search patterns.** Different customers search in different ways, and keywords self-organize into logical keyword groups. Each keyword group has a core keyword (e.g., "motorcycle insurance") with helper keywords (e.g., "quote," "rate," "cheap") plus some close synonyms (e.g., "motorbike," "moped," "Harley Davidson"). Do you know your keyword patterns? Are they reflected in your keyword worksheet?

- **Keyword Volume.** Smart SEOs fish where the fish are: they target keywords that have the highest search volumes. Have you researched which keywords have the highest volume in your industry, using the Google Keyword Tool or Keyword Planner?

- **Keyword Value.** It's not just about volume; it's also about value, especially value to you and your business. The Google Keyword Tool or Keyword Planner gives you useful data on the CPC (cost-per-click) bid on AdWords, but it's up to you to identify "riches in the niches," the very specific searches that are of high value to your sales funnel.

Your **keyword audit DELIVERABLE** consists of sitting down with management / your team and fleshing out an organized **keyword worksheet**. Then, measure your rank on Google to set a **baseline** of where your company stands in terms of target Google search queries.

▶▶ Deliverable: a Page Tag Audit

Now that you know your keywords, where do you put them? **Page tags**, of course. The easiest way to conduct a Page Tag Audit is by creating an Excel spreadsheet. (You can use our sample worksheet below). On the spreadsheet create a "tab" for each page of your website, then populate each "tab" with your comments about what the page already has in terms of SEO vs. what it needs as follows:

- **What is the logical keyword focus of each page?** Leaving aside the very special home page, each page on your website should have a tight, logical keyword focus. Conduct an inventory of all pages on your site, and cross-match each page to a logical, tight keyword query on Google that it can success-fully target. Next, audit whether the current tags contain the target keyword.

- **Meta Tag Audit.** The two meta tags that really matter, of course, are the TITLE and META DESCRIPTION tag. Inventory the existing tags vs. suggested improvements to the TITLE and META DESCRIPTION tags.

• **Tag Audit.** Besides the META TAGS, the A HREF, HEADER, and IMG ALT tags are important. Inventory your existing tags vs. the suggested tag improvements.

Having looked at tag structure, turn next to the **content** on the page. As we have learned, Google likes keyword heavy, redundant content that is written in high quality, natural syntax English. Inventory each page to verify that it has SEO-friendly content that matches the keyword target. If it does, great. If it does not, then you need to write that content!

A quick, efficient technique is to write a short (< 500 characters) keyword heavy paragraph about your company, products, and/or services and paste this paragraph on every page of the site. **Does your company have a "keyword paragraph" on every page in the footer?**

Then turn to missing pages. When comparing your keyword worksheet to your existing website, you may find that some keyword groups lack a matching page on the website. No bueno! Add these pages to your spreadsheet, and set a task of creating these new pages to match the target keywords or key phrases.

Note that if your page is template- or database-driven, you may have page "templates" and in that case you may just have to make changes at a template level to improve your tag structure for SEO.

Regardless, the purpose of the **Page Tag audit** is to compare / contrast your pages with SEO best practices to verify that your website has pages that "match" your priority keyword targets.

VIDEO. Watch a quick video tutorial on how to conduct a Page Tag audit at http://jm-seo.org/2999-j

Use the worksheet at http://bit.ly/pt-doc (Word) / http://bit.ly/pt-pdf (PDF) to produce your page tag audit **DELIVERABLE**.

▶▶ Deliverable: a Home Page Audit

The home page is the most important page of your website for SEO performance, so spend a lot of time working on your home page. A good home page audit works as follows:

Target Keywords. Reviewing your keyword worksheet, what are your most *important*, most *competitive* keywords? Use your powerful home page TITLE tag to convey to Google your website's primary keyword theme, and remember it must be less than eighty characters, with only about 66 visible on Google.

Meta Tags. Review and revise not only your TITLE tag but also your META DESCRIPTION tag, including high priority keywords and making sure that you respect the META DE-SCRIPTION character limit of 155 characters.

Home Page Content. Google pays a lot of attention to the text on your home page, so verify that the keywords on your keyword worksheet actually appear at least once on your home page. At the same time, do not clutter your home page so much that it doesn't look good "for humans." The art of SEO is to combine the keyword heavy text that Google likes, with the pretty visuals that humans like. This is especially true for the home page, so put pictures, graphics, and actions at the top of the page, and keyword heavy text for Google at the bottom.

One Click to Landing Pages. It should be "one click" down from your home page to your priority landing pages, so inventory whether a) your landing pages exist, and b) whether they are "one click" from the home page.

Use the worksheet at http://bit.ly/hpg-pdf (PDF) / http://bit.ly/hpg-doc (Word) to produce your home page audit **DELIVERABLE.**

▶▶ Deliverable: a Website Structure Audit

As we learned in the Chapter on Website Structure, there are do's and don'ts for structural SEO:

Do include keywords in your URLs. Are your existing URL's keyword heavy? Do your domains, directories, file names and even graphic names contain keywords?

Don't use parameter URLs. Inventory your existing URLs and look for question marks (?), percentage signs (%), and session IDs. All are very negative for SEO, and if they exist, have your webmaster or programmer transition to static or pseudo-static URLs as soon as possible.

Do sculpt your links. A strong SEO website uses internal link syntax to talk to Google. Your home page should have keyword heavy "one click" links down from the home page to your landing pages. Similarly, your site navigation should be keyword heavy and "sculpt" your links around keyword phrases.

Finally, make sure that your website contains your **Google friendly files**, especially a robots.txt file, an XML sitemap, and an HTML sitemap. Every page should link to the HTML sitemap, and the HTML sitemap in turn should have keyword-heavy links to all derivative pages. This important file makes it easy for the Googlebot to crawl your website.

Join **Google Webmaster Tools** to be part of the Google "Mickey Mouse Club" and get insider information on how Google perceives your website!

Remember to use the free worksheet at http://bit.ly/structure-pdf (PDF) / http://bit.ly/structure-doc (Word) to produce your website structure audit **DELIVERABLE**.

Now that you've completed these **DELIVERABLES**, it's time to move to our next step, **Step #4: Create Content.**

Content SEO

In **Step #1**, you defined your goals; in **Step #2**, you identified your keywords; and in **Step #3**, you structured your pages and website to talk to Google about your target keywords. In **Step #4**, you begin to populate your SEO-friendly website with keyword heavy content.

Content, after all, is king.

But let's be clear. Just throwing content up on your website willy-nilly won't help your SEO! Why? Well, for one, we've already learned that well structured content (SEO-friendly page tags, SEO-friendly website structure) is critical for success at SEO.

In **Step #4**, we will expand on this by creating an **SEO Content Marketing Strategy** ("Content SEO" for short) built upon your keyword targets.

Content SEO is all about creating web pages that match Google search queries with compelling, relevant content, be that on a specific web page, a press release, or a blog post. **Content SEO** is all about creating an on-going process (daily, weekly, monthly) of creating compelling SEO-friendly content for your website.

Let's get Started!

TO DO LIST:

>> Identify Keyword Themes

>> Create a Content Map

>> Deliverable: a Content Marketing Plan

>> Identify Keyword Themes

Every successful website has keyword **themes** just as every successful company or organization has a **focus**. You don't produce everything, nor do your target searchers search Google for everything. You **focus**, and they **focus**. If you are Safe Harbor CPAs (http://www.safeharborcpa.com), a CPA firm in San Francisco, for example, your target customers search Google for things like "San Francisco CPA Firms," "Business CPAs in San Francisco, CA," or keyword specific searches such as "CPA Firm for IRS Audit Defense in SF," or "FBAR Tax Issues 2013." Guess what? Safe Harbor CPAs has matching content on its website for each of those queries, and that's no accident!

If **keyword discovery** is about organizing your SEO strategy around keyword themes, then **Content SEO**, in turn, is about creating a strategy to produce the type of content that "matches" your keyword themes.

MATCH CONTENT
TO SEARCH QUERIES

The first step is to organize your keyword themes onto your keyword worksheet. Among the most common themes are:

Branded Searches. Searches in which customers already know your company, and simply use Google to find you quickly. In the example of Safe Harbor CPAs, a branded Google search is literally "Safe Harbor CPAs"

Anchor Searches. Searches in which a core customer need matches a core product. In the example of Safe Harbor CPAs, an anchor search would be "San Francisco CPA Firms," or "Tax Preparation San Francisco." For a large company like Progressive Insurance, the anchor searches are "Auto Insurance" or "Motorcycle Insurance."

Keyword Specific Searches. Searches that are usually (but not always) long tail searches (multiple search keywords), and reflect a very focused customer need. For example, "IRS Audit Defense CPA in San Francisco" or "motorcycle insurance quotes online" vs. just "CPA Firm."

News Searches. These are searches reflecting industry news, trends, and buzz. For example, with recent IRS initiatives to crack down on overseas assets, a search such as "2012 OVDP Program" reflects an awareness of the 2012 "Offshore Voluntary Disclosure Program."

These are not the only types of keyword queries that might exist; just the most common.

Many SEO content experts also distinguish between *evergreen* keywords (keywords that are always valuable such as "CPA San Francisco") vs. *time-sensitive* content (such as "2013 Tax Changes). And don't forget the difference between *educational* search queries and *transactional* search queries ("knee pain" vs. "best knee surgeon in San Francisco"). Finally, there is *link bait* content (such as infographics, or tutorial posts), designed to attract links, and of course *social media content*, especially content that is designed to be highly shareable on networks like Facebook or Twitter.

Regardless of the target keywords, the basic goal is to map out the types of content that are most relevant to you and your customers, and to start a content marketing process that generates highly relevant content on a regular basis.

Once your site is well optimized for SEO, you can often see the basic patterns directly in Google Analytics under Traffic Sources > Sources > Search > Organic. Here's a screenshot from the JM Internet Group's Google Analytics with each pattern with a yellow call-out:

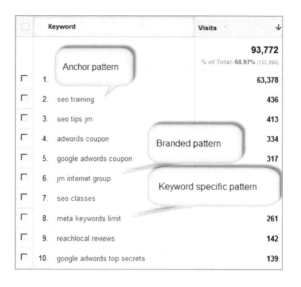

So the **anchor pattern** is reflected in "SEO Training" (a searcher looking for where he can find SEO training), the **branded pattern** is reflected in "JM Internet Group" (a searcher using Google to find the JM Internet Group), and the **keyword specific pattern** is reflected in "meta keywords limit" (a searcher seeking to understand the limits of meta tags).

In terms of the **news pattern**, here is data from Google Analytics on inbound search queries for "Microdata," a new type of data format for websites that became a hot topic in Spring, 2013:

	Non-paid Search Traffic	9
		% of Total: 0.01% (135,966) Site A
1.	microdata seo	4
2.	books on html5 microdata	1
3.	google seo microdata	1
4.	html5 microdata seo example	1
5.	tutorial html5 microdata for seo	1
6.	video microdata html5	1

For your first **TODO**, review your keyword worksheet, brainstorm your keyword patterns, check Google Analytics for keywords, then group your keyword families into patterns that reflect **branded**

search, anchor search, esoteric search, and **news search**. If there are other relevant patterns, indicate those as well.

▶▶ Create a Content Map

Now that you have your keyword themes, it's time to brainstorm the types of content you are going to create that will match the relevant keyword theme. Your second **TODO** is to create a **content map**. In a sense, you are "reverse engineering" the process of Google search: taking what people search on Google as your **end point**, and creating the type of content that has a good chance of appearing in Google search results as your **starting point**. Your **content map** will map your keyword themes to the relevant locations on your website.

Here are examples of how keyword themes are generally reflected on website locations:

Theme – Branded Searches
Location – *Home Page, About You, Testimonial Pages*
Branded search is all about making sure you show up for your own name as well as commonly appended helper words like "reviews." Make sure that at least some TITLE tags communicate your name, and your "about" page is focused on branded search. Don't forget branded search for key company employees (JM Internet Group vs. Jason McDonald, for example).

Theme – Anchor Searches
Location – *Home Page, Landing Pages, Product Pages (High Level)*
Anchor search terms generally reflect your product categories in the format that customers search. Revisit progressive.com, for example, and you'll see how each anchor search query is reflected in a focused landing page. In addition, the site navigation and links are "sculpted" around keywords to pull Google up to the target landing pages.

Theme – Keyword Specific Searches
Location – *Product sub pages, blog posts*.
Your esoteric searches are generally long tail searches, and/or searches for very niche, focused products or services. These are

less competitive than anchor searches and are well served by content on product sub pages as well as blog posts.

Theme – News Searches
Location – *Press releases, blog posts*
Every industry has news, buzz, and timely topics! The place to put this content is generally either in a press release on your website, and/or a blog post.

For your second **TODO**, take your keyword themes and map out where they should be reflected on your website into your **content map**. I recommend doing this in Excel.

In some cases, you may have *missing* elements (for example, you don't have a blog or don't produce press releases); in others you may have the elements there *already* (product specific pages, for example) but their content is not SEO-friendly (has poorly defined TITLE tags, content does not reflect logical keyword target, etc.). Regardless, you are mapping your keyword themes to the logical locations on your website with the goal of getting into a rhythm or content creation process of creating SEO-friendly content on a regular basis.

>> Deliverable: a Content Marketing Plan

Now that you have a **content map** of your website vs. your keyword themes on your **keyword worksheet**, you are ready to produce your **DELIVERABLE**: a **content marketing plan**. Your content marketing plan will consist of these basic phases.

Phase 1: Quick Fix. Based on your keyword worksheet including the content map, conduct an inventory of existing pages. Adjust their TITLE tags, META DESCRIPTION tags, and content to bring that content into alignment with your logical Google searches. I usually also write a "keyword paragraph" and place on all website pages to increase keyword density and allow for link sculpting. Don't forget to optimize the content of that all-important home page!

Phase 2: Structural Inventory. Are you missing anything? Often times, there will be a very important keyword pattern that has no corresponding landing page, for example. Or your site will not have a blog, or you will have never set up a press release system. Inventory what you are missing and start to prioritize what needs to be done to get that content on your website.

Phase 3: Content Creation Process. Once you have done the Quick Fix to the website and created any missing landing pages, set up a blog, and/or set up a press releases system, you need to create a content creation process. This is an assessment of who will do what, when, where, and how to create the type of on-going content that Google and Web searchers will find attractive.

WORKSHEETS. For your **DELIVERABLE** use the Content SEO Worksheet at http://bit.ly/cs-doc (Word) | http://bit.ly/cs-pdf (PDF).

Press Releases

After you've created your anchor or landing page content, press releases should be a major part of your **SEO Content** strategy. Why? Because Google rewards sites that have fresh content!

Here are the reasons. First, websites that have new, fresh content (for example, a press release or blog post put up in the last week) are clearly more "alive" than websites that never get updated. We live in a fast-paced world, and users want the *latest* iPhone software, the *latest* news about Obamacare, and the *latest* nutritional supplement. Google wants to give users the latest and greatest on any topic as well. Second, fresh content signals to Google that your website and business are still alive vs. the many "walking dead" websites that reflect businesses dead or dying in this age of recession. And third, press releases have a unique SEO advantage: **syndication**. Free and paid syndication services like PRLog.org or PRWeb.com connect with blogs, portals, other websites and even Twitter feeds to push your press releases across the Web, creating inbound buzz and backlinks which Google interprets as signs of community authority. Press release SEO, in short, gives a three-for-one benefit!

Let's get Started!

TO DO LIST:

>> Make a Press Release Calendar

>> Upload Your SEO-Friendly Press Releases

>> Leverage Free Press Release Syndication Services

>> Deliverables: Press Release Calendar and Your First Press Release

▶▶ Make a Press Release Calendar

What can make a good press release? **Almost anything**. Keep your keyword worksheet in mind and look for press release opportunities around your company. I recommend you create a **press release calendar** of opportunities.

For your first **TODO**, open up a Word document, title it "Press Release Calendar," and write down a list of possible press release topics and dates of the release. For example:

Sample press release topics and when to release:

> **Topic** – New Product or Service
> **Release** – Every time you have a new product or service, generate a press release.
>
> **Topic** – Annual Trade Show
> **Release** – Generate a press release before the annual trade show, as well as after announcing your participation to celebrate your success.
>
> **Topic** – Personnel Changes
> **Release** – Generate a press release for every major corporate hire.
>
> **Topic** – New website content
> **Release** – Generate a press release after any major blog post, list of "top seven resources," infographic, etc.
>
> **Topic** – Partnership Announcements
> **Release** – Generate a press release after any cooperative partnership with a company or supplier.
>
> **Topic** – Industry Awards or Milestones
> **Release** – Any time you win an industry award or cross a milestone (such as the 1000th follower on Twitter), it's time for a press release!

Your press release calendar will help keep you focused, and tie your press release opportunities to your keyword worksheet. The goal is to avoid writer's block and get into a rhythm of at least two press releases per month, minimum.

Once you have an idea in hand, here are the steps to create a press release:

1. Identify the press release idea. Realize that a press release can be not only a new product or a new technology but something as simple as your participation in a trade show, an event that you may be having, a new hire, new inventory, or even your commentary on an industry trend. Literally, anything new can become a press release!

2. Connect the press release idea to a target keyword from your keyword worksheet. The point of generating press releases, after all, is to improve keyword performance.

3. Create a press release using your SEO page template and follow "SEO best practices" for on page SEO (see below).

4. Upload the press release to your website, be sure that your website has a press release section with each press release on an independent URL, and include a "one click" link from the home page to the press release.

5. Leverage free and/or paid syndication services to proliferate mentions of your press releases around the Internet.

▶▶ Upload Your SEO-Friendly Press Releases

Double-check your press release to make sure that it follows "on page" SEO best practices. Here's your checklist:

Pithy, exciting headline
<TITLE> tag

First paragraph with "main idea"
<META DESCRIPTION> tag and first paragraph. Include a link to your website in the first paragraph usually around a keyword phrase.

Target URL
A target URL on your website, to which you want to attract Google. Embed this in the first paragraph, and have it as a "naked" URL (http://) format in the third paragraph.

Several paragraphs describing your news and an image.
Write keyword heavy copy and include at least one image with ALT attribute.

Contact information for more info.
Embedded URL early in the press release, set up in http:// format plus contact information at the end of the release

In other words, follow your HTML page tag template to optimize your press release in terms of its on-page SEO. Be sure to embed your target keywords in your <TITLE> tag, and use best SEO practices like the H1 family, <B>, <STRONG>, ALT attributes, for images etc. Write **keyword-heavy** text for the press release body! Make sure that it has a snappy <TITLE> and a snappy META DESCRIPTION / first paragraph so that people will be interested in "reading more."

At the website structure level, your best practice is to have a directory called "news" as in *http://www.yourcompany.com/news/* and to host each press release in HTML linked to from a primary news gateway page. I also recommend that you run at least three press releases on your home page, with "one click" links down to each new press release. All of this freshens your website and pulls Google into your new content.

Good examples of press releases can be found at http://www.jm-seo.org/news/ as well as http://www.qnx.com/news/.

VIDEO. Watch a quick video tutorial on how to write an SEO-friendly press releases at http://jm-seo.org/2999-k.

▶▶ Leverage Free Press Release Syndication Services

Once you've created your press release and uploaded it to your own website, you are ready to leverage press release syndication services. The best **free** service is PRLog.org (http://www.prlog.org/) and the best **paid** service is PRWeb.com (http://www.prweb.com/), owned by Vocus.

After you've set up your account on one of these services, open your press release in one browser window. In another window, log into the press release syndication service and begin the process of submitting a release. Copy and paste the following from your press release into the syndication service -

Headline. Make sure it includes your target keywords!

Quick Summary. Write a pithy, exciting one-to-two sentence summary. This will usually become your META DESCRIPTION tag on the syndication service.

News Body. Copy and paste your news body. Be sure to embed a URL after the first or second paragraph, and write in the simple http:// format (since embedded links may not be retained in syndicated press releases).

URL / Active Link. Make sure that your press release has at least one prominent link to your website. News is especially good at getting Google to index new web pages on your site!

Contact Information. Include a description of your company with a Web link and email address for more information. This is another link-building opportunity.

Tags. Select appropriate tags for keyword / content issues as well as target geographies.

Finally, commit to publishing press releases on your website and using news syndication on a regular, consistent basis. It's better to publish one release per month, consistently, than six releases in one month and nothing for six months.

WORKSHEETS. Use the press release worksheets at http://bit. ly/news-for-seo (Word) or http://bit.ly/uTjLoo (PDF).

VIDEO. Watch a quick video tutorial on how to syndicate press releases at http://jm-seo.org/2999-l.

A warning about the Penguin Update. Google's latest anti-SEO effort has been called the "Penguin Update." The Penguin Update specifically targets low quality link schemes, meaning many inbound links to your website from low-quality sites that often have the same keyword phrase with a link. The take-away is to not overdo press release SEO! First, don't issue more than two to three press releases per month via paid syndication services such as PRWeb.com. Second, don't overdo the use of keyword-heavy links in the press releases. If you sell "online insurance," don't issue press release after press release with the phrase "online insurance" linking back to your site. Instead, I recommend that you vary your inbound links as follows:

Branded Links. Have about 1/3 of your press releases linking to your company name.

Naked Links. Have about 1/3 of your press releases linking only to an http:// formatted link (no keyword links / no branded links).

Keyword Links. Have about 1/3 of your press releases linking to keyword phrases, but vary these phrases and do not over do them! For instance, have one press release syndicated that links to "online insurance," and another that links to "online motorcycle insurance," and still another that links to "top company for insurance online."

Post-Penguin the goal is to have a "natural" inbound link footprint consisting of branded, naked, and keyword heavy links. Even a few "click here" links are good to throw into the mix.

▶▶ Deliverables: Press Release Calendar and Your First Press Release

The first **DELIVERABLE** for this chapter is your press release calendar. This can be as simple as a Word document or Google document that serves as an "idea list" of when to generate a press release. The goal is to avoid writer's block and get into a rhythm of generating at least two press releases per month. The second **DELIVERABLE** is your first SEO-friendly press release, uploaded to your own site and pushed out via a syndication service such as PRLOG.org or PRWEB.com.

Blogging

Nothing is as easy or as powerful for SEO as blogging! While landing pages reflect your anchor keyword terms, and press releases can build inbound links via syndication, blogging allows you to sculpt content for more narrow keyword specific queries as well as to respond quickly to industry buzz and trends. In addition, frequent blogging - like frequent press releases- sends a powerful signal to Google that your website is "fresh." Every website should have a blog!

Let's get Started!

TO DO LIST:

>> Make a Blog Calendar

>> Set Up Your Blog for Best SEO

>> Write SEO-friendly Blog Posts

>> Deliverables: Blog Calendar and Your First Blog Post

>> Make a Blog Calendar

Today's SEO ecosystem heavily rewards sites that blog on keyword-heavy topics. Blogging without knowing your keywords is an exercise in sheer vanity, whereas blogging with keywords in mind is a powerful tool to get you to the top of Google. Moreover, your blog can connect to your social media strategy as a "long read" to complement the "short reads" on Twitter, Facebook, or Google+. A good blog post gives you something to "point people to" on social media.

As an SEO Content strategist, look around your company and identify blog topics as well as other company employees who can contribute to the blog. Unlike press releases, blog posts can be much more informal, opinionated and quick. So whereas you might generate just two press releases per month, set a goal of at least one blog post per week, if not more.

You cannot overblog! As long as your blog content is fresh, original, and keyword-heavy, all blogs posts will help your SEO. The more the merrier!

Depending on your company, a blog calendar can help you keep track of possible blog topics and themes.

Here is a sample blog calendar for a hypothetical roofing company in Dallas, TX.

Sample Blog Topic: We complete a roofing job.
When To Post: Write a blog post about each roofing job, when completed, with information on the city where the job was located, the type of roofing material used, and customer reaction. Goal is to help with geo-targeted searches.

Sample Blog Topic: Our day-to-day in a host city for a job.
When To Post: Because geographic search terms are important for a roofing company, create city-specific blog posts such as your favorite "taco joint" in the city, or variances in city roofing codes.

Sample Blog Topic: Industry trends and events
When To Post: Any time there is an industry trend, such as a new roofing material, chime in with your own opinion. Ditto for any industry events or events in your Dallas, Texas, area.

Sample Blog Topic: New website content
When To Post: Blog about your own website, explaining what new content we are creating and why.

Sample Blog Topic: Partnership Announcements
When To Post: Identify potential blog opportunities with our partners.

Sample Blog Topic: Industry Awards or Milestones
When To Post: Any time you win an industry award or cross a milestone (such as the 1000th follower on Twitter), it's time for a blog post!

You'll see many similarities between successful SEO blogging and SEO press releases. The difference is one of degree: blogging is quicker, more informal, and more a quantity play vs. the more formal, higher quality status of press releases.

>> Set Up Your Blog for Best SEO

The best blog platform by far is WordPress (http://wordpress. org). But regardless of your platform, follow these basic principles for successful SEO blogging:

Host your blog on your own site. Blogging helps with site freshness vis-a-vis Google as well as acts as link bait. So it makes little sense to host your blog on another site. If at all possible, host your blog at your own domain in the position of http://www.company.com/blog.

Check each blog post for good SEO. As you write a blog post, check to make sure that your blogging platform allows for basic "on page" SEO: a keyword heavy TITLE tag, META DE-SCRIPTION tag, the use of the header family, one image with the alt attribute defined, and keyword-heavy cross-links.

Make sure your blog allows for keyword heavy tagging and cross-indexing. Make sure that your blog allows you to "tag" a post with keywords and that these "tags" act as URL cross-links.

Verify that your blog URLs are keyword heavy. Numeric, parameter-centric URLs are very bad for SEO, so make sure that your blog generates keyword-heavy URLs for each post.

At the home page level, a best practice to have "one click" links from your home page down to at least three, rotating blog posts. If you are running WordPress, be sure to install the Yoast SEO plug in (http://yoast.com).

Many people do not correctly "tag" each blog post, yet tagging is incredibly important to SEO-friendly blogging! Make sure that your blog tags match your keyword themes, and make sure that when you write a blog post each post gets tagged. One of the better blogs to emulate is by Nolo press (http://blog.nolo.com). Here's a screenshot of the tags at the bottom of the page for a post on bankruptcy forms:

WordPress has two types of tagging: "categories" and "tags." From an SEO perspective, both accomplish the same thing: lumping your posts into SEO-friendly cross-linked URL's. Both are strongly encouraged because both give Google an SEO-friendly URL structure to grab onto. Here's a link to the Nolo blog "bankruptcy" tag: http://bit.ly/nolo-br. Notice how the practitioners at Nolo are churning out blog post after blog post on their keyword theme of bankruptcy and related keywords! And notice the URL structure itself, which mimics the target keywords and signals to Google that this blog has quite a bit of content on bankruptcy: http://blog.nolo.com/bankruptcy/tag/bankruptcy-2

⏩ Write SEO-friendly Blog Posts

Blogging is a complementary SEO content strategy to your anchor landing pages, your home page, your product pages, and your press releases. Whereas anchor landing pages focus on your evergreen anchor keyword terms, your blog can focus on more keyword specific, timely topics. Blogging is especially useful for posting content that responds to quick industry trends. Here are the steps to writing a good blog post:

1. Identify the target keywords. A good blog post is laser focused on a very narrow keyword, so do your keyword research first!

2. Follow "on page" SEO best practices. Make sure that your post follows all of the "on page" rules such as a keyword heavy TITLE, META description, etc.

3. Consider an action or purpose. Have a defined action for each blog post, usually by embedding a link from the blog post "up to" one of your defined anchor landing pages. Another use of blog posts such as "Top Ten Things that Can Go Terribly Wrong at Your Wedding" is link bait; people will link to informative, provocative, shocking blog posts.

4. Tag your blog post. Identify keyword themes for your blog that match those of your keyword worksheet and recognize that each blog post is part of a keyword cluster, supporting the entire website's SEO themes.

VIDEO. Watch a video tutorial on SEO-friendly blogging posts at http://jm-seo.org/2999-m.

▶▶ Deliverables: Blog Calendar and Your First Blog Post

The first **DELIVERABLE** for this chapter is your blog calendar. This can be as simple as a Word document or Google document that serves as an "idea list" of when to generate a blog post. The goal is to avoid writer's block and get into a rhythm of generating at least one blog post per week, if not more. The second **DELIVERABLE** is your first SEO-friendly blog post, uploaded to your own site and tagged with appropriate (keyword) tags.

Links

Steps #1 to #4 are all internal. They are to-dos that you control just as you control the job you want and the resume you build to (hopefully) get a job. In **Step #5**, we cross the Rubicon, shifting our attention to the actions of others through "off page" SEO. References matter for a job search, and external links matter a great deal for SEO.

Step #5 in the **Seven Steps to SEO Success**, therefore, is to "go social." Google pays incredible attention to how others talk about your website, whether in the format of inbound HTML links or inbound social mentions. We'll turn first to **links**, the more traditional of the two, and in the next chapter look directly at **social mentions**.

Remember that a link *from* a directory, blog, web portal, or other industry site to your website is counted as a **vote** by Google that your site is important. The more links (votes) you have, the higher you show on Google search results for your target keywords. But how do you get links? In this chapter, we outline the basics of effective link building for SEO.

Let's get Started!

TO DO LIST:

>> Define Your Link Objectives

>> Solicit the Easy Links First

>> Identify Directory, Blog, and Other Link Targets

>> Reverse Engineer Competitors' Links

>> Create Link Bait

>> Deliverable: A Link Building Plan

>> Define Your Link Objectives

In-bound links are worth their weight in gold, but not all links are created equally. Your first step in link-building, therefore, is to define your link objectives. The best links enjoy the following attributes:

- **Good Syntax** - the best links have good syntax with your "keyword / keyphrase" nested inside the <A HREF> tag as in <A HREF="http://www.yoursite.com/">your target keyword</A>

High Authority (PageRank) - the best links come from high PageRank websites inside your keyword communities.

- **Sheer Quantity** - the best links occur in substantial quantities. More is better.

Most companies have more than one keyword community or "link neighborhood" as it is often called in the SEO industry. If you are a Bed and Breakfast in Boston, Massachusetts, for example, then you "live" in at least two keyword communities: a) Boston, Massachusetts websites, and b) websites in the B&B industry. Using your keyword worksheet brainstorm the various keyword communities in which you can solicit links.

At a technical level, the `rel="nofollow"` attribute tells Google to ignore a link; these types of links are deprecated by Google. So if you see that in the HTML source code it's a sign that given link is not as valuable. However, many nofollow links such as those from relevant social media profiles like Yelp or YouTube clearly do impact SEO. My feeling therefore is that all links have some value including even nofollow links from social media sites and relevant blog comments.

Just like in real-world elections, the most important part of successful link building is sheer **quantity**. Politicians don't always sweat the small stuff; they kiss a lot of babies, and shake a lot of hands in their quest for high quality votes. So should you in your quest for links!

POLITICIANS KISS BABIES
SEOS GET LINKS

▶▶ Solicit the Easy Links First

Your ecosystem partners, i.e. those companies you do business with on a daily basis, are your easiest link targets. If you attend an industry trade show as an exhibitor, for example, ask for a link back to your company website from the trade show website. If you buy a lot of stuff from a supplier, require a link back to your company website from their website as a condition of doing business. If you sponsor a local charity like the Breast Cancer Walk Pittsburgh, ask for a link back to your company website from the charity website. If your boss teaches a class at the local university, help him set up a link from his profile page back to your company website. If anyone on your company gets interviewed or is able to write a guest blog post on another website, make sure that they get a link back in their author profile!

You get the idea: create a **culture of link solicitation** in your organization, so that on a day-in and day-out level everyone in your company is soliciting links, and (over time) getting them.

Don't forget your **social media profile** links! If local search is important to you, make sure that your company is included in Google+ Local, Yelp, Citysearch and other local listing sites. Be sure to set up a Twitter, Google+, Facebook and other social media profiles for your companies and include links in those profiles.

Don't forget your **directory links**! If your industry has industry-specific directories, make sure you are included in those directory listings with links.

Your first **TODO** is to open a Word document, title it "Easy Link Targets" and create a list of your easy ecosystem partners and other link targets.

▶▶ Identify Directory, Blog, and Other Link Targets

Directories, blogs, and other websites found on Google make great link targets. How do you find them? For **directories**, do a Google search for keywords such as "AddURL + Your Keywords," "Directory + Your Keywords," and/or "Catalog + Your Keywords." As you browse these sites, make note of their **PageRank** and keyword themes that align with your own target keywords. Use the Solo SEO link search tool (http://bit.ly/link-search) for a quick and easy way to look for possible link targets.

To find **blogs**, type your target keywords into the Google search box, and then use the pull-down tab for "More," and select "Blogs." Browse blogs that cover your keywords, make note of their PageRank, and create an Excel spreadsheet of each blog with the appropriate contact person.

Finally, do searches for your major keyword phrases. As you search, segregate your **direct competitors** (sites so similar to your own that there is no way that they would link to you) from your **complementary competitors**. These are sites like blogs, personal websites, portals, directories, Wiki entries and the like that "show up" on your searches but may have a complementary reason to link to you. A wedding photographer, for example, might find not only directories of wedding suppliers but also florists, priests, caterers, bakers, and facilities that would likely exchange links due to the complementary nature of their businesses.

Your second **TODO** is to open a Word document, title it "Directory Targets" and create a list of your directory, blog, and other types of complementary websites for link building.

▶▶ Reverse Engineer Competitors' Links

Many free fabulous tools exist to "reverse engineer" inbound links of competitors. Your objective is to identify complementary websites that link to a competitor but who may also be willing to link to you. Type each competitor's home page URL into these tools, and then surf to the appropriate websites, making note of the PageRank, content, and contact information for your "Link Building" target list. Here are my three favorites:

Open Site Explorer (http://bit.ly/open-explorer). Type your competitor's home page into this tool, or the URL of a highly ranked site on Google. Browse to see who is linking to your competitor.

AHrefs (http://ahrefs.com). Similar to Open Site Explorer, this free tool allows you to input a competitor URL and reverse engineer who is linking to that competitor.

LinkDiagnosis (http://bit.ly/link-diagnosis). Sign up for your free account, input a competitor's home page URL, and let this tool do the hard work for you. This tool will identify the PageRank of link targets plus tell you if the NOFOLLOW tag is in use, and it even allows you to export your data into an Excel report - all for free!

Here's a screenshot of Open Site Explorer's analysis of http://www.progressive.com/ showing that that site has over 8000 linking domains totaling to over 43,500 inbound links. No wonder progressive.com dominates searches for insurance

OPEN SITE EXPLORER

http:// www.progressive.com/

⊕ compare up to 5 sites

Domain Metrics:	Page Metrics:		Just Discovered Links
Domain Authority	Page Authority	Linking Root Domains	Total Links
85/100	88/100	8,096	43,586

Inbound Links	Top Pages	Linking Domains	Anchor Text

⊘ Shazzam! We've updated our inbound link filters a bit to clarify which links are being shov

VIDEO. Watch a video review of the Open Site Explorer tool at
http://jm-seo.org/2999-n.

At the end of this process, you should have a defined list of "link
targets" sorted by PageRank and their keyword themes with your
"keyword community." Your third **TODO** is to take this list, and
then go one by one through the results, soliciting links from the
various targets. If summer is here, this is a great task for a cheap
intern!

>> Create Link Bait

Link bait takes link building to the next level. Link bait is the art
of creating content that is so compelling that people will *spontane-
ously* link to it, without you even having to ask. Have a customer
of the month contest (if your customers have websites), have a
supplier of the month award (if your suppliers have websites).
Email, call, and even give gifts to blogs, portals, and other content
sites that might be willing to cover you and your company. In link
building, remember you are dealing with other people, so look at
the situation from their perspective: what's in it for them?

Your **blog** can be great link bait. Write the definitive article on
"top ten new technologies" for your industry, write a provocative
blot post on why "such-and-such" is a "terrible" idea to stir

controversy, share an emotional story. Blog posts that are informative, controversial, or emotional tend to get shared, and linked to, the most.

Consider creating **badges:** customer of the month, best tool for such-and-such, partner companies, verification of a certification test, and so on and so forth.

Have you ever noticed how many Yelp results show up high on Google search? Have you ever thought of how many companies have Yelp badges on their websites, with links up to their Yelp listings? Consider being the "Yelp" of your industry via badges. Here's a screenshot giving an inside look at how Yelp promotes its link juice via badges:

If you have a programming budget, create **widgets** such as BMI calculator, the real-time price of gold, a reverse mortgage calculator. Any sort of free tool or widget that is relevant to your industry can be link bait to bring in links in a spontaneous way. Infographics are another way to get links: create an informative, humorous, outrageous or shocking infographic and let the links roll in!

Your fourth **TODO** is to have a company meeting and brainstorm possibilities for link bait. If so, create a step-by-step plan to implement your link bait strategy.

▶▶ Deliverable: A Link Building Plan

The **DELIVERABLE** for this chapter is a link strategy document. This can be as simple as a Word document or Google document that serves as an "idea list" of your link building strategies and targets with the easiest, most common first and the more difficult, more infrequent targets last.

> **WORKSHEETS.** Use the link-building worksheets to define a link-building strategy for your website. For our worksheets, go to http://bit.ly/link-word (Word) or http://bit.ly/link-pdf (PDF).

Social Media

A topic unto itself, Social Media has many SEO implications. **Social mentions** - that is the posting of your URLs on sites like Twitter, Google+, Facebook and more - is a new kind of link building. Having robust **social profiles** (like an active Twitter feed or active Google+ account) signals Google and its search algorithm that your company is active and important. Indeed, Google+ presents unique SEO opportunities, starting with the Google +1 button, proceeding through Google+ corporate accounts, and ending with authorship via a Google+ profile. SEO is going social, so in this chapter, we explore the brave new world of **Social Media SEO**.

Let's get Started!

> **TO DO LIST:**
>
> **>>** Understand Social Media SEO
>
> **>>** Get Social Mentions!
>
> **>>** Set up Robust Social Profiles
>
> **>>** Get Google+: Google's Favored Social Network
>
> **>>** Deliverable: A Social Media SEO Plan including Google+

>> Understand Social Media SEO

Links, as we have seen, count as votes in SEO. Google clearly rewards sites that have many keyword relevant links (especially those from high authority websites), with higher positions on Google search results. Social Media in a sense builds on this network of link authority. How so? While Google has not publicly clarified how it uses what are called *social signals* in SEO, we can postulate some logical patterns of how Google might interpret social signals. Indeed, many efforts in social media SEO will certainly *not hurt* and *may probably help* one's SEO performance, so there is little downside and a lot of upside in "going social" with your SEO strategy!

How does social media impact SEO?

First and foremost, sites that enjoy **inbound links via social mentions of URLs** from social sites like Twitter, Google+, or even Facebook are clearly topical and relevant to Google. A simple *site:twitter.com* search on Google reveals over one billion indexed Tweets, and a simple *site:facebook.com* search on Google reveals over six billion indexed Facebook posts. Google clearly pays attention to the social sharing of links!

Second, robust and active **social profiles** are another obvious clue to Google of your website's relevance. Many sites link out to their Yelp account, Google+ profile, Twitter account, Facebook page, LinkedIn page, etc., and those social sites can be indexed by Google. Google can clearly "see" how active your company is on social media, how many "followers" you have, and whether those followers, in turn are active. It stands to reason that having an active social media footprint, with active posts and many engaged followers is a new signal to Google about your website's relevance. Indeed, much of this is keyword centric, another reason why knowing your keywords is paramount to SEO success!

Third, social search has made the Web more **human**. Whereas in the past, the creators of Web content were relatively invisible, new ways of communicating "microdata" can tell Google how many reviews your site has, who the content author is, and whether this author has an active, engaged follower community or not. Realizing that SEO is now a **social game** positions your company for not just the present but the future of SEO success on Google.

▶▶ Get Social Mentions!

Getting **social mentions** of your URLs is a lot like traditional link building. First, look for easy social mention targets. Ask customers, suppliers, and ecosystem partners to tweet your URLs, share your company's blog posts on Facebook, and to "+1" your URLs. Second, "reverse engineer" competitors or use common Google and social media searches to find social media sharers who might be interested in your content.

For example, to find people Tweeting on your keywords, go to https://twitter.com/search-advanced, type in your competitor names or your keywords and look for Tweeters who have a) many followers, and b) tweet on your keyword themes. Then reach out to them and encourage them to tweet your latest blog post, press release, or informative new widget. Here's a screenshot showing a search for tweets on "organic food":

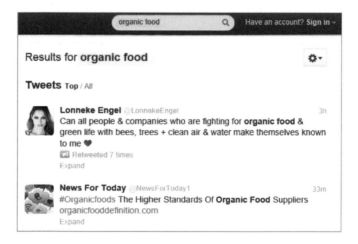

Similarly, you can find heavy **Google+ sharers** by doing a Google search *site:plus.google.com* and your keywords. Click on "search tools" and then set your time horizon to the "past week" for the freshest shares.

Here's a screenshot of that search, looking for people active on Google+ sharing content on "organic food":

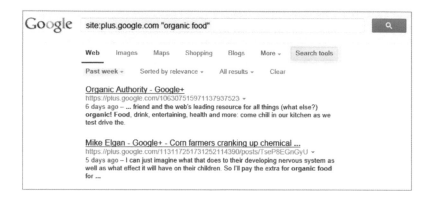

Google, in particular, is a great way to search other social media sites for heavy sharers. Try Google searches like *site:facebook.com {your keywords}*, *site:linkedin.com {your keywords}*, *site:pinterest.com {your keywords}*, etc. to identify site-specific individuals who are good targets to share your own content.

Topsy (http://topsy.com) is another excellent search engine of social shares. Don't forget blogs! Go to Google, type in your keywords, click on the more button and select blogs. Then click on search tools and past month. Here's a screenshot of a Google blog search for posts in the past month on "organic food":

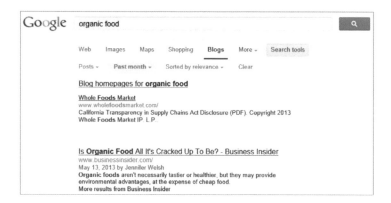

Your first **TODO** is to open an Excel document, title it "Social Sharers" and create a spreadsheet with columns for the social network , account name, number of followers, and common keyword themes for each. If you don't have a lot of time, concentrate on the social network that is most applicable to your industry and the most keyword relevant social sharers who have the highest number of followers.

▶▶ Set up Robust Social Profiles

It's a no-brainer that Google looks for companies with active social profiles. Given two companies competing for a top position on Google, one with thousands of people circling its Google+ corporate page, and another without a Google+ corporate page at all, to whom do you think Google is going to give top placement? This same fact probably goes for other social networks as well, especially open ones like Twitter or Pinterest. For each, be sure to fill out your company profiles with relevant keywords and cross-link from each social profile to your website. Leaving aside Google+, here are the most important for most companies with links to their business help guides (if available):

Facebook (https://www.facebook.com/business)

Twitter (https://business.twitter.com)

LinkedIn (http://bit.ly/li-business)

YouTube (http://www.youtube.com)

Pinterest (http://business.pinterest.com)

Once you set up a profile, be sure to populate it with your relevant keywords and cross-link it back to your website. Be sure to also link from your home page to your social networks to make it easy for Google to see which website corresponds to which social network. All of the networks have easy to use badges that enable these important cross connections; just look for badges in the relevant business help center as listed above.

Finally, as you post content to a social network, keep your keywords in minds, grow your fan base, and encourage interactivity between you and your fans. Social media is a two-for-one benefit: first, the *direct* benefit from the social media platform itself as you engage with users, and second, the *indirect* benefit as Google "observes" how popular you are and feeds that data into its SEO algorithm.

Your second **TODO** is to create each relevant social profile for your business, cross-link to your website, begin to post interesting content, and encourage followers.

▶▶ Get Google+: Google's Favored Social Network

Guess who owns Google+? **Google!** Guess who owns search: **Google!**

Think about what that **cross-ownership** means for SEO.

Imagine you were a bunch of Google executives trying to figure out how to grow Google+ vs. competitors like Yelp, Facebook, or Twitter. Might you think of ways to leverage your near monopoly in search to incent companies to get on board with Google+? For example, what if you made it pretty clear that having a robust participation in Google+ and growing social presence on Google+ would improve a company's rank on Google organic searches? Do you think Google could be that cynical?

We'll leave that aside, but it's clear that participating in Google+ is certainly not going to hurt your SEO and there is a great deal of evidence that it does, in fact, help it (a lot).

GET
GOOGLE+!

Google+ is actually not one but three different social networks:

Google+ Profiles. These are the profiles of individuals on Google+, real people sharing content on Google+ about their lives and favorite websites.

Google+ Business Pages. These are the business pages on Google+, the Fords, Toyotas, and Whole Foods corporate accounts by which businesses promote their wares and connect with customers.

Google+ Local Accounts. These are business accounts, similar to those on Yelp, that focus on local search.

And finally there's the Google +1 button (http://www.google.com/+1/button) (someone "votes" for your website as cool and shares it with his or her friends on Google+) and the Google +1 badge (https://developers.google.com/+/web/badge), which is a quick way for someone to click from your website to your Google+ corporate account and thereby "circle" you. Get, and enable both of these for your website!

We'll look at Google+ Local in detail in the next chapter, so let's start our examination of Google+ with the **Google+ Business Page** first. This is essentially the same concept as business pages on Facebook. You set up a business page, people "like" you ("circle" you), and thereby when you share messages on Google+, they will see these messages in their news feed on the Google+ social network. From an SEO perspective, being active on Google+ at a business or corporate level probably helps your SEO. It also has a big impact on your branded search terms. Once properly enabled, a branded search for your company name will generally activate your Google+ corporate account in the far right of the search screen. Here's a screenshot for the search "National Geographic" showing their Google+ corporate page at the right:

Heretofore, there isn't a lot of real activity on Google+, so I don't recommend spending a lot of time on Google+ for business. Just set it up, enable it, and feed it many of the same posts you're hopefully already doing on Facebook and/or Twitter. You can learn more about Google+ Pages for business at http://bit.ly/biz-gplus.

Your third **TODO** is to set up a Google+ Business page for your business, cross-link to your website, begin to post interesting content, and encourage followers.

Next, let's turn to Google+ at an individual level. In contrast to business pages, **Google+ Profile** pages for individuals offer a **huge** benefit for SEO. I strongly recommend you make having a robust Google+ Profile for your company's CEO a top priority!

Why?

When correctly tied to the website, a strong Google+ Profile enables **authorship**, and can get your picture to show on relevant Google searches. Here's an excerpted screenshot for the Google search "seo class" showing my picture on the SERP results page:

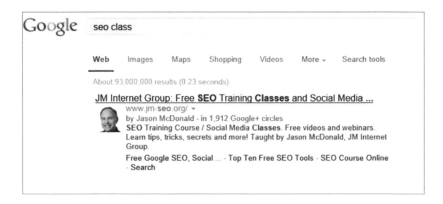

Having the picture show makes you stand out on the Google screen, and encourages your personal brand. In addition, you can nurture a "virtuous circle" whereby showing up on Google gets you more followers, and behind the scenes having more followers on Google+ gets you higher search results. Before long, you are the guru of your industry, how cool is that?

Google's Matt Cutts has explicitly stated that they are paying attention to authors on Google+ and their cross-linked content. (You can watch his YouTube Video at http://bit.ly/matt-cutts-ga).

You can't find a clearer signal that if you want to succeed at SEO you need to enable Google+ authorship!

The steps to enable Google+ Profile / Authorship are:

1. Set up a **Google+ Profile** for the relevant person.

2. Populate the "**about**" section of the Google+ Profile with relevant keyword-heavy text.

3. In the "**contributor to**" section of the Google+ Profile cross-link your website or blog.

4. On the every page of the website for which you want the picture to show on Google add *rel=author* attribute to the end of the link back to the relevant Google+ profile.

Your picture won't generally show until you have about twenty followers. The process is a little complicated, so I created a step-by-step tutorial and video.

VIDEO. Watch a video tutorial on Google+ Profiles and authorship at http://jm-seo.org/2999-0.

▶▶ Deliverable: A Social Media SEO Plan including Google+

The **DELIVERABLE** for this chapter is a Social Media SEO plan including Google+. Remember, we are not talking about social media, in general, but rather about the specific use of social media to bolster your SEO performance!

WORKSHEETS. Use our worksheets to conceptualize your Social Media SEO plan, go to http://bit.ly/sm-seo (Word) or http://bit.ly/smm-seo-pdf (PDF).

Local SEO

Many Google searches are local in nature. Searches like "pizza," "divorce attorney," or even "marketing consultants" tend to have a local nature, and Google is pretty good at inferring which searches have a local character. Users in turn often append geographic terms to their Google searches such as "NYC" or "SF" to clarify to Google that they want "Watch Repair NYC" rather than "Watch Repair by Mail Order" and so forth and so on. So if you have a clearly local business (a roofing company, a CPA firm, a watch repair shop, a personal injury law firm, a hypnosis practice...), **local SEO** is a must.

Even if your business isn't entirely local, local can still be quite relevant. And, local SEO crosses into **review marketing** which is an area in which social media and SEO overlap.

Let's get Started!

TO DO LIST:

>> Understand Local Search Opportunities

>> Claim and Optimize Your Local Social Media

>> Cross-link Your Website to Your Local Social Media

>> Create a Review Marketing Strategy

>> Deliverable: A Local SEO Plan

>> Understand Local Search Opportunities

Local search is huge on the Internet. People search for "Dallas Roofer" or "Hypnotherapist New York City" or even just

"Sushi."Conduct an inventory of your search keywords and note which queries produce prominent Google+ Local results. Searches for **single** or **short tail** keywords such as "Sushi" or "Divorce Attorney" often produce localized results; take note of which single or short tail searches are especially relevant.

Second, keep an eye out for other services like Yelp or Citysearch popping up prominently in your local search results. Review your keyword worksheet and designate those searches (usually the short tail searches) that trigger Google+ Local results. You can tell if Google is "going local" because you will see a list of two or more companies with their addresses on the search results page. Here's a screenshot for "Italian Restaurants" with location set to Tulsa, Oklahoma:

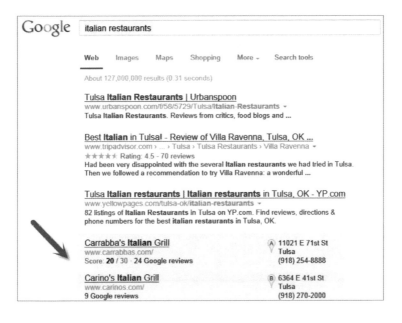

Notice also how the #1 and #2 results are urbanspoon and tripadvisor.com, themselves listing services of local businesses. It's not Google **OR** local search services like urbanspoon, Yelp, or tripadvisor. It's Google **AND** these search services for effective local SEO!

Even for other types of searches, you can still see localized results. With your location set to Tulsa, OK, for example, a search for "SEO companies" brings the following listing to position #2:

Tulsa **SEO Firm** | SEO Tulsa | SEO Tulsa OK - Seed Technologies
www.seedtechnologies.com/Tulsa-**SEO**.aspx ▾
Search Engine Optimization. As one of the largest Tulsa SEO firms, we employ a staff
of both internet marketing specialists and web designers that enable us to ...

Note that you can **set your search location** by clicking on Search Tools at the top right of the Google screen, and then typing in any city in the United States. Now, change your location to San Francisco by clicking on Search Tools at the top right, and seed-technologies.com disappears to be replaced by alchemistmedia.com.

San Francisco SEO – Alchemist Media **SEO Services**
https://www.alchemistmedia.com/ ▾
by Jessie Stricchiola
We do SEO. In San Francisco. SEO Strategy, Quick Reviews, Ongoing SEO
Management & Consulting.

Clearly, Google is localizing the search query "SEO Company" just as it does "Pizza" or "Divorce Attorney." So for many, many search patterns, local SEO is a must! Pay close attention to how the Google results change as you vary your local city.

Your first **TODO** is to revisit your keyword worksheet and identify those search queries that generate **local results** on the Google SERP results. This identifies the search patterns for which you really need to focus on local SEO tactics, to which we now turn.

▶▶ Claim and Optimize Your Local Social Media

Your second **TODO** is to claim your local listings. Start with **Google+ Local** (http://www.google.com/places) and follow the instructions to claiming your listing there. Be sure to claim your listing with an email address and Google account that is a corporate asset, as you **cannot** transfer a Google+ Local listing from one user to another!

> **VIDEO**. Watch a video on how to find and claim your Google+ local listing at http://jm-seo.org/2999-p.

Once you've claimed your listing, be sure to optimize it by writing a keyword heavy 200 character description and choosing relevant categories for your business.

Beyond Google+, **find, claim,** and **optimize** your other local listings across the major sites. Here's a list of the most important sites for social media at a local level:

> **Citysearch** (http://www.citysearch.com)
> **Bing Places** (https://www.bingplaces.com)
> **Yelp** (http://biz.yelp.com)
> **CitySearch** (http://www.insiderpages.com)

A nifty service that attempts to locate all of your relevant local listings is GetListed.org (http://getlisted.org)

▶▶ Cross-link Your Website to Your Local Social Media

Once you've successfully claimed a listing, it's time to cross-link your website to your listing. Your third **TODO** is to cross-link the website to the listing URLs. Your listing should also have a) the **same** address as on your website, and b) a **link** to your website. Now, you are doing the reverse: linking from your website to your local listings.

Remember: use the same address and same phone number consistently across all the local listing sites as well as your own website.

Preferably on your home page, or at least on your "about" or "contact us" pages, add a link from your website to the direct listing address. The local listing URLS can be quite long and you must get them exactly correct. Here is the Google+ Local listing for the JM Internet Group:

> https://plus.google.com/115873218478122623127/about

Here's the Yelp listing for Ron Gordon Watch Repair:

http://www.yelp.com/biz/ron-gordon-watch-repair-new-york-2

And if you look at the bottom of http://www.rongordonwatches.com you'll see the following paragraph which has a) a consistent New York city address, and b) a link to the relevant local listing sites for Ron Gordon Watch Repair:

> Ron Gordon Watch Repair is located at 280 Madison Ave, Ste. 510, New York, NY 10016. Our NYC watch repair service provides professional watch repair service throughout New York City (NYC), Manhattan, Midtown Manhattan, Downtown and the boroughs of New York, NY. Read our Google+ Local, Yelp Reviews, Insider Pages, and City Search Reviews, online. Come visit our professional watch repair shop in New York, NY, today! We also service and repair watches online, especially vintage watches. Follow Ron Gordon on Google+!

By using a consistent name, address, and phone number across your listings and by cross-referencing them to each other, you help Google "see" which website goes with which listings. Make it easy for Google to localize your website, and Google will reward you with better rankings.

>> Create a Review Marketing Strategy

Reviews matter! The more reviews you have from people in your local community, people who use your target keywords in their reviews, and people who are active reviewers, the more Google will propel your website to the top of its local search results. Reviews are, in fact, a lot like links and Google clearly rewards websites that have more reviews.

After claiming and optimizing your local listings, your next **TODO** is to create a review marketing process. *Encourage* your happy customers to review your business in every way possible – on Google, on Yelp, on Citysearch, and on any other local listing site important to you.

For review marketing:

- Make sure that at the **end of a successful sale**, your customer is politely asked to review you on Google Places, Yelp, Google Merchant Center (Google Shopping), etc. Make "Please review us!" part of your sales process.

- Think of using **real-world promotions** to encourage reviews such as stickers, cards, brochures at your place of business that ask people to "review you" on social media sites.

- Use **follow up emails** with customers as well as social media like Facebook to thank people who have already reviewed you, and to encourage people who might.

Remember that, technically speaking, it is a *violation* of terms of service to solicit paid reviews, so encourage reviews in a judicious and polite manner!

The challenge is that if you don't ask for reviews, generally speaking you'll get reviews from only your unhappiest customers. The reality is that if the meal is good and the atmosphere fun, we don't rush home and write a review of the restaurant, whereas when the meal gives us food poisoning and the service is horrible, we are likely to fire up the computer, log on to Yelp or Google+ Local and let the owner have a piece of our minds.

Encouraging positive reviews in a judicious manner is a critical part of local SEO!

▶▶ Deliverable: A Local SEO Plan

The **DELIVERABLE** for this chapter is a local SEO plan. This can be a simple Word document or Excel spreadsheet listing the searches for which Google returns local results, your available local listing services such as Google+ Local or Yelp, the listing status (claimed or yet-to-be-claimed), and some action items for your staff towards a review encouragement strategy.

WORKSHEETS. For relevant worksheets, go to http://bit.ly/ smw-doc (Word) or http://bit.ly/smw-pdf (PDF).

Metrics

Google Analytics is the best free Web metrics tool available today. It is, however, only a tool. Before you even start with Analytics, your first step is to think through what you want to measure. Common metrics are your rank on Google for target keyword queries, which data queries get traffic to your website, other ways people find your website, and whether landings on your website convert into goals, such as registrations or sales. Second, after you've identified what you want to measure, you need to turn to not just Analytics but other metrics tools and understand how to use them. They're not easy to use! Third, there are even more advanced techniques that can "slice and dice" your data so that you truly know what's going on with your website.

Let's get Started!

TO DO LIST:

>> Define Your Metrics Goals

>> Measure Your SERP Rank and PageRank

>> Use Google Analytics Basic Features

>> Use Advanced Features in Google Analytics

>> Deliverable: Google Analytics Worksheet

>> Deploy Circular Analytics for Improved SEO

>> Define Your Metrics Goals

Metrics, especially as seen through the prism of Google Analytics, can seem overwhelming. For most companies, there are just three basic things to measure: rank on Google, traffic sources, and user behavior. Only the latter two can be measured via Google Analytics. Here is a breakdown:

1. Your Rank on Google Searches and Google PageRank. SEO starts with whether your website is in position 1, 2, or 3 on Google or at least page one. In addition, you should measure your Google PageRank or Web authority over time. Neither of these important variables can be measured in Google Analytics directly.

2. Traffic Sources. Learn how people *find* your website, especially your best performing keywords and referrer websites.

3. User Behavior. Learn what people do once they land on your website, especially marketing goals such as registrations or completed sales. Understand *successes* and *failures* and investigate ways to improve the success rate.

When designing your website for effective SEO, I recommend you identify a few concrete **goals**. Typical goals for most website are:

Registration. Getting potential customers to fill out a registration form usually for a "free consultation," "free webinar," or other "free" offer. The object is to get a sales lead (name, email, phone number).

Purchase. Getting potential customers to actually buy a product. This is typical for less expensive products that people might buy direct from your website.

In both cases, after the person completes the "action," they should get a "thank you" form. In Google Analytics, this "thank you" becomes codified as your "goal" and can be measured vs. incoming web traffic, or clicks, as a "conversion."

▶▶ Measure Your SERP Rank and PageRank

Your **SERP rank** (Search Engine Results Page) measures your website's position on a target search query. For instance, JM-SEO.org's rank for the Google query "SEO Classes" is typically No. 1. Your **PageRank**, in contrast, is a measurement of your authority on the Web. As we learned in link building, think of your PageRank as a measurement of how important your site is on the Web.

To measure your SERP rank, the best free tool is Rank Checker by SEOBook (http://www.seobook.com). The tool is available only on Firefox. After installing it, go to Tools > Rank Checker > Options and set the "delay between queries" to 99 seconds. This is because if you run a long keyword list, Google will stop providing rank data to the tool. Then to run the tool from Firefox, go to Tools >Rank Checker > Run > Add Multiple Keywords. Enter your domain and keyword list, hit start and the tool will measure your rank on Google and Bing.

Here's a screenshot of the tool for searches relating to SEO Training, Atlanta, GA. Just a random example of the JM Internet Group in top positions for SEO training searches:

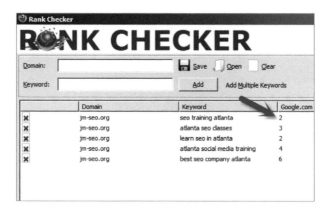

Another great rank measurement tool is from Sitemapdoc.com (http://bit.ly/uJmJMt). With their tool, you can measure your rank on any query one at a time, instantly.

Your first **TODO** is to revisit your **keyword worksheet** and input your rank for target sample phrases. I usually create a tab called "sample keywords" and measure my rank on Google keyword queries before I start an SEO project, after I have implemented the "on page" changes, and every month therafter. I then look for ranks **greater than ten** as bad, **greater than three** as in trouble and work on those priority keywords.

VIDEO. Watch a video on how to use the Rank Checker tool at http://jm-seo.org/2999-p.

Secondarily, I recommend you measure your inbound links as a surrogate for Google PageRank on a monthly basis. Go to Open Site Explorer (http://www.opensiteexplorer.org), input your website home page URL, and note the four metrics at the top of the page: domain authority, page authority, linking root domains, and total links. Record each of these on your keyword worksheet each month. Here's a screenshot for jm-seo.org:

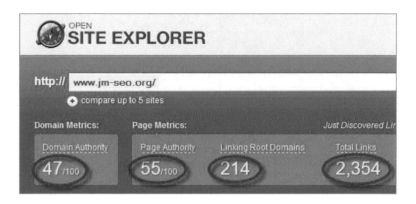

Domain Authority is a surrogate for *Google's PageRank*, which you can measure with the Google toolbar but the reality is that Google's public data on your *PageRank* is notoriously unreliable; hence, I recommend a surrogate indicator such as Open Site Explorer's *Domain Authority*.

>> Use Google Analytics Basic Features

Now that you have a measurement of your SERP rank vs. target keywords and your domain authority out of the way it's time to turn to Google Analytics. Google Analytics is a powerful, and free, metrics tool suite available at http://www.google.com/analytics. Log on to create your free account. The first and most important step is to download and install the **Javascript tracking code**. Following the instructions at Google Analytics, and place this code in the <HEAD> tag at the top of each and every page on your website. (For a Google tutorial on how to do this, go to http://bit. ly/ga-tracking).

Once you have installed the Javascript code on your site and allowed enough time to elapse for data to accumulate, it's time for some basic Analytics.

- Click on Standard Reports, Audience, to see basic data about how many visitors are coming to your website daily, where they are coming from, and basic traffic sources such as search engines vs. referring sites.

- Click on Traffic Sources, Sources, Referrals and browse "referring" sites such as blogs, portals, news releases, etc., that are sending users from their website to yours via clicks.

- Click on Traffic Sources, Sources, Search, Organic, and then Keywords (on the right) to see which keywords and key phrases are performing well for you in generating incoming web traffic.

- Click on Content, Site Content, and then Landing Pages and Exit Pages to see the most popular pages for entering and exiting your website.

VIDEO. Watch a video on how to determine inbound organic Google searches in Google Analytics at http://jm-seo. org/2999-q.

Basic Analytics provides you a lot of key information on incoming web traffic. The keywords data is especially interesting. Look for patterns to your keywords and ideas for generating new website content such as blog posts or news. Finally, you can click on the date field at the top far right of Analytics to change the date filter for data or to compare two time periods.

▶▶ Use Advanced Features in Google Analytics

Beyond Basic Analytics, there are advanced features in Google Analytics that you do not want to miss. First, click on **Advanced Segments** to "slice" and "dice" your data based on criteria such as "new visitors" vs. "repeat visitors" or the geographic locations from which visitors come. You can save any Advanced Segment and use it as a filter throughout Analytics. Set up an Advanced Segment, for example, by geographic area, and then click back to **Traffic Sources** to see which keywords worked better for you in that particular geographic area.

Many people don't realize that they should click on the Advanced Segments tag. Here's a screenshot with the tab highlighted in yellow:

Second, set up "Goals" for Analytics by registering your "Thank you" page after a registration or purchase. To do this, go to the primary log in page on Analytics by click on the "Admin" icon in the top right of the page. Next, click on your profile name (usually your website URL). Then click on "goals" in the middle of the page. Here is where you define a "goal" and a "funnel," which is the steps taken to reach the goal. In Advanced Analytics, you can therefore see not only how people get to your website but the steps that take as they click through your website.

> **VIDEO.** Watch a video on how to set up goals in Google Analytics at http://jm-seo.org/2999-r.

Once a goal is set up, you can go back to the main page in Google Analytics, and use Advanced Segments to slice and dice your data and thereby see what traffic is converting (i.e., completing your goal) vs. what is not.

Finally, don't miss some of the free official Google videos available for learning more about Analytics such as Google Analytics IQ Lessons (http://bit.ly/conv-u). Ironically, that Analytics IQ

Lessons are nearly impossible to find or get to from inside of Google Analytics. That's Google for you!

▶▶ Deliverable: Google Analytics Worksheet

The **DELIVERABLE** for this chapter is a completed worksheet on Google Analytics. Sit down with your management, marketing team, and web team and identify what you'd like to measure, who's going to measure it, and where you are going to store that data.

WORKSHEETS. For relevant worksheets, go to http://bit.ly/ga-doc (Word) | http://bit.ly/ga-pdf (PDF)).

▶▶ Deploy Circular Analytics for Improved SEO

Analytics coupled with rank measurement gives you powerful data about how you stand on Google for your target keywords, what keywords work for you in generating incoming clicks, and what people do on your website once the arrive. As with a physical fitness program, your metrics objective is to measure **before, during,** and **after** your SEO efforts.

Google calls this "circular analytics," whereby you measure not only how people get to your website but how they "convert" into Goals. Then you theorize new changes to your website such as new landing pages, new structural arrangements to content and text, new offers such as "free consultations" or "free events," and measure your success rate vs. your bounce rate. Your goal with circular analytics is to improve your SEO by a constant process of experimentation and measurement. In SEO, as in all things, success takes constant effort!

Good luck!

Learning

SEO is a competitive game that never stops evolving. The Google algorithm changes and adjusts, user behavior evolves, and your competitors also improve their SEO skills. Recently, for example, the aspects of social media have become ever more important, as has localization and personalization issues. All require the successful practitioner of SEO to adapt.

"Never stop learning" must be your motto! In this chapter, I point to resources to help you be a life-long learner.

Let's get Started!

TO DO LIST:

>> Download the Free Companion SEO Toolbook

>> Use the Worksheets, Resources, and Quizzes

>> Bookmark and Read SEO Media Resources

>> Download the Free Companion SEO Toolbook

The SEO *Toolbook* is a companion to this *SEO Workbook* and contains hundreds of free tools, organized by the Seven Steps. To get your free copy, just go to http://www.jm-seo.org promo and enter the password: seoworkbook. On the landing page, just click on the relevant link to download the **SEO Toolbook** in PDF format.

⏩ Use the Worksheets, Resources, and Quizzes

Throughout this SEO Workbook, I have referenced helpful worksheets, videos, and resources. These follow the Seven Steps methodology and can be accessed at http://www.jm-seo.org/promo and enter the password: *seoworkbook*. That landing page will also give you access, chapter by chapter, to quizzes to test your own knowledge.

⏩ Bookmark and Read SEO Media Resources

SEO changes frequently, so I urge you to pay attention to Google directly as well as the many wonderful blogs that cover search engine optimization. Those are available in the SEO *Toolbook*.

In addition to the companion SEO *Toolbook*, I produce a free **SEO Dashboard**, listing the top, free learning resources for staying up-to-date on SEO.

To get the free *SEO Dashboard*, all I ask is that you write a candid review about *SEO Fitness Workbook* on Amazon.com. Then, simply go to the URL below, follow the instructions, and you'll receive access to my *SEO Dashboard*, my launch pad to the best SEO tools and media resources I use on a daily basis.

- http://www.jm-seo.org/offer

If you have any problems, email me at info@jm-seo.org or call 510-713-2150 for help. Good luck!

~ Jason McDonald, Ph.D.

Made in the USA
Lexington, KY
20 October 2013